Thank you),

♡ Gideon

GIVING

a HANDBOOK *to* HAPPINESS

for THE MODERN PHILANTHROPIST

Gideon Bernstein, CFA, CAP

ISBN: 978-0-578-33159-1

To my parents,
Richard & Leah Bernstein
who taught me the value of
a life fulfilled through giving

Contents

Foreword 6

Introduction 9

Chapter 1: Giving it Away 11
- What is Philanthropy?
- The Simple Joy of Giving
- Anyone Can Be a Philanthropist
- What Kind of Philanthropist Are You?
- The Power of Anonymous Giving

Exercise: What are your motivations and values?

Chapter 2: The Personal Side of Giving 41
- How Giving Can Help Fulfill Your Life
- Giving After Suffering a Loss
- Giving and the Ultra Wealthy
- Anyone Can Make a Difference

Exercise: The simple joy of one-to-one giving

Chapter 3: Barriers to Giving 68
- The Paradox of Giving
- The Scarcity Effect
- The Bystander Effect
- Never Enough
- Too Many Choices
- Analysis Paralysis

Exercise: Narrow your focus areas

Chapter 4: Strategies for Giving 106
- Creating Impact
- Types of Giving
- Vehicles for Giving
- Timeframes for Giving
- Smarter Giving
- Picking the Right Tool

Exercise: Tackle the nitty gritty

Chapter 5: From Moment to Movement 159
- Spread the Fire!
- Inspire the Next Generation
- Pay It Forward
- Give All Year Long
- Get Vocal
- Just Ask
- Create a Movement

Exercise: Make your own giving pledge

Afterword 187
Acknowledgements 191
About the Author 193

Foreword

I'll never forget the day in early 2018 that Gideon and a group of volunteers from the Jewish Community Foundation of Orange County arrived at Second Harvest Food Bank of Orange County to pack food boxes in memory of Gideon's son Blaze who had been tragically murdered just weeks before. I was leading the organization at that time and often saw hundreds of volunteers in a single day, but that night was particularly special as I witnessed the beginning stages of a movement to #BlazeItForward—to encourage acts of kindness in honor of Blaze.

I've since had the opportunity to get to know Gideon and his wife Jeanne, and have been inspired by their work to turn an unthinkable situation into good, not only for our Orange County community, but also for our world. They are inspiring thousands of people around the world to show up, to give their time, talent, and treasure, and to amplify kindness through their #BlazeItForward movement.

It's no surprise that Gideon has written a book about giving. He has been involved in philanthropic causes for many years, and his passion for making giving a foundational pillar of one's life has only continued to grow. He is a 'giving evangelist,' which is the direct good that has come out of his heartbreaking loss of Blaze.

Whether you are new to giving or just need a more strategic approach to philanthropy, Gideon's book provides clear and practical advice that you, your family, and your professional advisors can use to make giving a more fulfilling experience and to create greater impact.

In my 25 years working as a leader in the nonprofit sector, I'm often in awe that some of the most generous givers are those who may not appear, at least on the surface, to have the most wealth. These are individuals who simply want to make a difference and take action to make positive change a reality. What stands out to me most poignantly about these individuals is that they experience a greater sense of happiness and joy because they make giving a priority.

It's been the honor of my career to have accepted gifts of all sizes from all types of givers—individuals, corporations, and foundations. Seeing the joy of these givers as they proudly hand over a gift to support a mission they care deeply about is a true thrill. No matter the size of the gift, I always feel a huge sense of responsibility to use the funds wisely, maximize their impact, and then report the positive impact that was made back to the giver. The bottom line is that while giving blesses those in need, it blesses the giver even more.

I've also personally witnessed the power of giving in my own family. I grew up with a single mom who struggled to make ends meet, and I saw how my family members, my church, and community organizations supported us through the years to make sure we stayed afloat. And I saw how my mom, with very limited resources, still gave of herself generously as a volunteer and donor to our church and other causes. While I've met some of the wealthiest and most generous people throughout my career, my mom is the most powerful example of giving I will ever know.

As I learned from my mom, giving isn't just something you do when you've reached a certain level of income. It's a lifestyle. It's a way of living that will always bring joy to you and hope to others—no matter the size of the gift. This book provides an opportunity to have important conversations with family members, friends, co-workers, and clients about the responsibility we each have to make this world a better place for future generations—and there's no more powerful way to do that than through giving.

Nicole Suydam
President & CEO, Goodwill of Orange County

Introduction

I wrote much of this book in the early days of the coronavirus pandemic in 2020. Little did any of us know when we rang in the New Year on December 31st that we would all be required to 'shelter in place' and stay at home for more than a year—or that the Delta variant would further delay our return to normal far into 2021 and beyond.

So many people across the globe lost loved ones, and everyone who survives this era will forever be affected by its impact. Jobs were lost. Businesses were shuttered, in many cases permanently. Governments around the world took desperate measures to keep society functioning. The situation was far beyond anything we could have comprehended until we were in the thick of it.

Luckily, we were able to find silver linings in this strange new world. Isolation forced us to contemplate the meaning of our lives—to think deeply about what was important, and to remember how precious each life is. COVID-19 also served as a global call to help others. Never have so many individuals taken personal, immediate action to try to save jobs, save lives, and support frontline workers. Calls to action permeated social media. Remote concerts (without live audiences) were held to raise funds. Billionaires funded private jet delivery of N-95 masks and ventilators to hospitals. At a time when so many people were in need, the concept of giving became one of the unifiers of our society during one of the most polarizing eras in recent times.

This book was written to remind everyone, everywhere of the importance of giving—and to provide insights and strategies to encourage people of all levels of wealth to continue to give and make an important difference in this world long after the coronavirus is behind us. During the pandemic, giving meant delivering a hot meal or groceries to the elderly like my wife did... or, like Elon Musk, flying your corporate jet to China to pick up enough masks to save hundreds of thousands of lives in Ohio.

The pandemic, of course, represents just one important moment in time. But make no mistake: the needs of our global community will always be evolving, and there will always be people hurting and causes that need your help. There will always be a reason to give *now*.

One thing I learned from my own experiences during the pandemic is how to be more present. Forced to sit still, I found time to stop and smell the roses. I became more mindful of how much I really love my family, my wife, my dog, and my home. I am more aware of how deeply I care about humanity—and that, despite our tribal instincts, we all share the same DNA. And I see clearly how important it is to shift our mindsets and treat each other as one global family.

I'm not alone in these reflections. Over the past 18 months, I've seen many friends and clients gain a new sort of enlightenment, asking themselves, "What do I want to do for the rest of my life? How can I make a difference that matters?" I hope this book helps you answer those questions for yourself—and that it inspires you to make the act of giving a part of your life's mission.

Gideon Bernstein

CHAPTER 1

Giving it Away

"People will forget what you said,
people will forget what you did,
but people will never forget
how you made them feel."
— *Dr. Maya Angelou*

If I told you I had the secret to happiness, what would you say? What if I told you that this secret has been confirmed by individuals all over the world and by top neuroscientists?

It's true. I do have the secret to happiness.

The secret is *giving*.

It's simple. It's powerful.

And it will change your life.

What is Philanthropy?

It's a weighty word, isn't it? Philanthropy. Just hearing it conjures up images that seem vastly distant from our current lives. It's easy to picture characters straight out of an episode of Downton Abbey, all being served by their staff as they lounge on overstuffed sofas, sip brandy, and ponder the best way to bestow their vast fortunes on the needy.

I'm not sure that image was ever accurate, but even if it was, philanthropy—or charitable giving, or simply *giving*—looks completely different in the here and now. Not only have the ways we can give expanded (think GoFundMe, Facebook donations, or donating to offset your carbon footprint), but there are also fewer limitations on who is doing the giving. In the 21st century, anyone can be a philanthropist.

Including you.

Despite the fact that the way we give has changed, the definition of philanthropy remains the same. If you Google philanthropy, the first definition that pops up is this one from Merriam Webster:

phi·lan·thro·py | \ fə-'lan(t)-thrə-pē \
plural **philanthropies**

Definition of *philanthropy*

1   : goodwill to fellow members of the human race
     especially : active effort to promote human welfare

2   **a**   : an act or gift done or made for humanitarian purposes

      b   : an organization distributing or supported by funds set aside for humanitarian purposes

Goodwill. Human welfare. Humanitarian. All of these are key attributes of philanthropy. The actual origins of the word, however, may do an even better job of explaining what true philanthropy is all about.

Etymologically, philanthropy comes from the Late Latin word *philanthropia* and the Greek word *philanthrōpia*, which both mean "kindliness, humanity, benevolence, love to mankind," and from *philanthrōpos*, which means "loving mankind, useful to man." Aeschylus, the Greek playwright, is credited with bringing those words together to coin the term we know today—*philanthropy*—more than 2,500 years ago.

Centuries later, philanthropy is still used to describe generosity in all its forms. A philanthropist is someone who gives their 'time, talent, and treasure' to help make life better for other people. In other words, philanthropy is all about performing acts of kindness, humanity, and love for the people and the causes we care about most.

But it's about so much more.

Are philanthropy and charity the same thing?

The difference between philanthropy and charity may come down to simple semantics. In general, 'philanthropy' is considered to be a more strategic, long-term approach to giving that spans years, decades, and even generations. 'Charity' is typically used to refer to a single act of giving to a specific person, group, or cause.

Whatever you choose to call it ("a rose is a rose is a rose" after all!), what matters most is choosing to give.

One reason philanthropy can feel so grandiose is because of the sheer power it wields and the magnitude of impact it can create. The act of giving is extremely potent. It's also highly personal. When you choose to give, you become an active agent of change in the world. That is true no matter how many resources you have to share—or how few. If you give, no matter what you give, you are officially a philanthropist. You are proactively taking personal responsibility for shifting *something* in the world.

The Simple Joy of Giving

Giving can be uniquely rewarding because acts of philanthropy often provide an immediate feedback loop that allows you to see exactly how your action creates change. And yet this action isn't entirely selfless. While it's true that giving, by its nature, requires us to give something up (money, time, resources), it is often emotionally rewarding for the giver. Knowing that you are doing something to make the world even a little bit better doesn't just *seem* to feel good—it actually creates a positive biological response.

Back when I studied psychology in college, I was fascinated by the mechanics of the human brain. I loved exploring how our choices can change our physiology, and how our physiology can change how we think and how we feel. I learned that though we tend to view our brains and our actions as separate, that's not the reality at all. This scientific fact plays a role in many areas of our lives—including in the act of giving.

In October 2020, the *New York Times* ran a story about a 'happiness class' at Yale University taught by psychology professor Laurie Santos. Titled 'The Science of Well-Being,' the class had just claimed the spot as the #1 most popular course at Yale. When Yale offered it for free online, millions of people around the world jumped at the opportunity to hear what Professor Santos had to teach about what drives happiness from a scientific standpoint, and what changes we can make in our lives to effectively rewire our brains to be happier. When asked to sum up her teachings, Santos said this:

> "We assume that self-care looks like a nice bubble bath—or even hedonistic pursuits, selfish pursuits. But the data suggests that the right way to treat ourselves would be to do nice things for other people. We actually get more out of being more open and more social and more other-oriented than spending money on ourselves. It's a bigger increase to your happiness."

Santos found a way to package the information in an appealing way and Yale gave her the perfect platform to share the news, but the idea and the research that supports it is not new. Over and over again, science confirms that the simple act of giving can help improve your mood, increase your sense of purpose, reduce your stress levels, improve your health, heighten your sense of connection to others, and make you happier.

Science confirms the joy of giving

In a 2007 study by NIH's National Institute on Aging (NIA) and the National Science Foundation, researchers at the University of Oregon used functional magnetic resonance imaging (fMRI) to look at how specific regions of the brain are activated during acts of giving. The study found that when people chose to give part of a new stash of money to charity rather than keeping it all for themselves, that

action activated regions of the brain asso-
ciated with pleasure, social connection, and
trust, creating a 'warm glow' effect.[1]

The study was simple, but telling.

At the start of the study, each participant
was given $100, and they were told they could keep what-
ever money remained at the end of the session. For the
next hour, an fMRI scanner was used to look at brain
activity while participants viewed a series of possible
money transfers to a local food bank on a computer
screen. In some instances, participants could decide
whether to accept or reject the donation. In others, donations were required, with a percentage of the participant's
stash being transferred automatically. In other cases,
money was unexpectedly added or taken away from the
account of either the participant or the charity.

The fMRI brain scans showed that each scenario—receiving money, seeing money automatically go to a good
cause, or deciding to donate money—activated similar
pleasure-related centers in the brain. Scientists believe
that this type of behavior releases endorphins in the brain
to produce what is known as the 'helper's high.'

It's no wonder so many people choose to give... even
when giving comes at a personal cost.

---

[1] Brain Imaging Reveals Joys of Giving, National Institutes of Health, June 2007

In the US, we're fortunate to live in a society that offers financial incentives for giving. While the federal tax code is constantly changing, it continues to support deductions against income, capital gains, and estate taxes for charitable contributions. During the pandemic, tax incentives were included in major economic relief bills that provided additional 'above-the-line' tax deductions for charitable gifts. Tax benefits like these have long served as important motivations to encourage giving.

But they can also create angst for some givers. It's not uncommon for charitably minded people to question whether it's right to receive a financial perk for donating money to a cause. While I'm sure philosophers could debate the issue ad nauseam (and are likely discussing it at this very moment), the upside of a tax incentive is that it puts more money back into the pockets of those who give—which enables them to give even more. If the whole idea of tax incentives doesn't sit quite right with you, rethinking the purpose of incentives can help. Rather than looking at tax incentives as a quid pro quo, try thinking of them as a way to enrich your power to give. Every dollar you 'save' in taxes is another dollar you have to give to others.

Giving offers unexpected rewards, but the greatest reward of all is the knowledge that you are taking action to make the world a better place. By giving your time, money, or resources to support something aligned with your personal values, you are taking action to create real change.

The Giving Tree

In Shel Silverstein's classic story *The Giving Tree*, a tree "loved a little boy very, very much—even more than she loved herself." As the boy grows, the tree gives him more and more. Leaves to play with. Branches to swing from. Shade to lie in. As he grows, she gives him every-thing she has to offer. Apples to sell. Branches to build a house... and wood to make a boat and sail away.

In the end, all that is left of the tree is a small stump, which she offers to the boy—who has become an old man—as a place to sit and rest. "And the tree was happy."

When my kids were young, I had to explain why, after giving everything, the tree was happy. But for anyone who has given generously and made a difference in the life of another, no explanation is needed. We are the lucky ones who know that the giving itself is our reward.

And we are happy.

Anyone Can Be a Philanthropist

"If you think you are too small to make a difference,
try sleeping with a mosquito."
— *Dalai Lama*

One of the most wonderful things about philanthropy is that anyone can be a philanthropist. You don't need to be Bill Gates or Warren Buffett! No matter how much or how little you have to give, you already have everything you need to make a difference. Having wealth may make giving easier, and it can certainly increase the level of impact you're able to achieve. But the act of philanthropy—of giving—can be done by anyone, anywhere, regardless of status or net worth.

Anyone can be a philanthropist, and anyone can make a difference.

Philanthropy is deeply personal, and it can take on many forms. You can make a monetary gift to support a cause that matters to you. You can also practice philanthropy by giving your time, talent, or resources to help others. An act of philanthropy can be as simple as giving money to a homeless person, or as complex as creating a private foundation to support causes that are selected and managed by a board of trustees.

In both cases—and everywhere in between—creating a personal giving strategy can help you become the most effective philanthropist you can be.

Giving in the age of coronavirus

COVID-19 became a household word and a global nightmare in 2020. While it will likely take years to assess the actual economic impact of the pandemic, it's clear that individuals and families were hit hard, both emotionally and financially. And yet, according to a report from Indiana University's Women's Philanthropy Institute (IU-PUI WPI), 56% of households in the US engaged in charitable giving during the pandemic to help their neighbors through the crisis. According to the report, one-third of US households donated directly to charitable organizations, other individuals, or businesses.[2]

Despite widespread economic insecurity due to the coronavirus, people in the US continued to give, and not in monetary donations alone. Almost half of households surveyed, 48.3%, engaged in other types of charitable giving, such as ordering takeout from local restaurants, purchasing gift cards from small businesses, or continuing to pay for services orders like house cleaning and daycare that were unused due to shelter-in-place orders.

---

[2] "COVID-19, Generosity, and Gender: How Giving Changed During the Early Months of a Global Pandemic," IUPUI Women's Philanthropy Institute, Indiana University, September 2020

How people chose to give during the pandemic shifted,
but the act of giving continued—even during a global crisis.

The pandemic brought out the philanthropist in many. People I know continued to pay their housekeepers, nannies, and hairstylists during the lockdown, even when they couldn't use their services. Neighbors helped neighbors by grocery shopping, dog walking, and weekly check-ins with the elderly. I serve on the Board at an organization that 'gave' to others by suspending membership fees during the pandemic. At a more public level, hundreds of top music groups—including Dave Matthews Band, Sofi Tukker, and the Grateful Dead—offered free live stream concerts. Cellist Yo-Yo Ma launched a social media movement called 'Songs of Comfort' that featured online collaborations of musicians, singers, dancers, and all sorts of entertainers. It seemed that people everywhere were giving what they could. Together, we witnessed something beautiful amidst the isolation, loneliness, and fear.

There is no single, correct way to be a philanthropist. By making informed, thoughtful decisions about how to give, you can pave a path that is meaningful to you and enables you to deliver the greatest possible impact.

Anyone can do it.

What Kind of Philanthropist Are You?

"Life isn't just about taking in oxygen
and giving out carbon dioxide."
— *Malala Yousafzai*

One of the first steps in becoming a philanthropist in the 21st century is determining the kind of giving that fits your style. What motivates you to give? What are your attitudes and beliefs about giving? What is your giving personality? No matter what kind of philanthropist you may be, understanding the different types of philanthropy can help you narrow your options, find your focus, and begin to build your own philanthropic mission.

Here are some of the most common types of philanthropy. Which ones resonate with you?

■ Community Philanthropy

Like other types of philanthropy, community philanthropy includes giving time, money, or resources to support others or create change. What makes it different is that it specifically includes gaining the support of local citizens, leveraging the knowledge and experience of community members, and identifying non-community resources that can help address certain challenges or help improve the quality of life in a community. It focuses on empowering community members to control what happens in their community—including using assets and skills within the community, building trust through participation and collaboration, and sharing decision-making throughout the process. Organizations that practice this community philanthropy include Amazon Partnerships Foundation, Community Foundation for South Sinai, and the Jewish Community Foundation Orange County.

■ Devout Philanthropy

Many religions promote the ideology of giving and supporting the needy. In the Jewish faith, *tzedakah* is the practice of giving away 10% or more of your earnings to care for those in need. The Christian faith calls this practice *tithing*. In the Muslim faith, it is referred to as Zakat. In each case, the practice is an obligation to give a percentage of your income or cumulative wealth as part of your faith. While some churches ask that these 'gifts of the faithful' are donated through the church itself, for others the act of giving is completely personal, giving individuals the choice of how, where, and when to give. Judaism, Christianity, and Islam all recognize two levels of giving: obligatory giving and additional voluntary giving.

Giving by millennials

Inherited wealth is a huge topic today. The reason: millennials are poised to come into more money than any prior generation thanks to their Baby Boomer parents. According to a recent study by Coldwell Banker Global Luxury® program and Wealth Engine[3], the coming Great Wealth Transfer will put more than $68 trillion into the hands and bank accounts of millennials.

The report also revealed that millennials are generous with their money. 35% of those surveyed have donated to charities, regardless of their level of wealth, and among millennial millionaires, that number jumped to 56%. Not only are they more likely to give than prior generations, but they are giving in different ways than their parents and grandparents. As true 21st century philanthropists, millennials are passionate about aligning their giving with their personal values, and environmental and political causes top their charitable priorities.

As 'the impact generation,' millennials hold the financial power and the philanthropic drive to shape the world.

---

[3] "A Look at Wealth 2019: Millennial Millionaires," Coldwell Banker, October 2019

■ Venture Philanthropy

When John D. Rockefeller III coined the phrase 'venture philanthropy' back in 1969, he described it as an "adventurous approach to funding unpopular social causes." Not much has changed since then. Today, venture philanthropy continues to be focused specifically on social causes, using venture capital financing strategies to raise funds. Venture philanthropists are usually founders, officers, or board members of charitable startups or charitably focused organizations that want to support causes that are relevant to the mission of the organization. Robin Hood Foundation, the Cure Alzheimer's Fund, and the Danone Communities are great examples of venture philanthropy in action.

■ Environmental & Social Philanthropy (ESG)

The environment has become a hot spot of philanthropic giving in recent years. As the impact of climate change has increased, the need for money to support environmental issues has become urgent. Environmental philanthropy aims to address this need by focusing on giving time and money in support of environmental issues, specifically through non-governmental organizations. Another thing that makes ESG different is that, while most more traditional forms of philanthropy—such as philanthropic foundations that focus on issues like the arts or education—are structured to spread out giving over many years, ESG organizations are usually structured as 'time-limited' or 'spend-down' foundations, with the goal of spending all their assets within 20 years. This approach has become increasingly popular in the past decade as modern-day philanthropists follow the model of the Bill & Melinda Gates Foundation that was designed to spend all its resources within 20 years of the Gates' deaths. (Happily, the foundation has remained united despite the couple's divorce in 2021.)

The spend-down approach in action

The AVI CHAI Foundation is
another example of a foundation that used a 20-year spend
down approach. Founded by
Sanford Bernstein, much of
the Foundation's mission was

achieved through a grant-making program that began in
1984 and was completed as scheduled in 2019. (Note that
Sanford Bernstein has no relation to me; he is the name-
sake of the NY securities firm Sanford C. Bernstein & Co.
which was sold to Alliance in 2000.)

At a philanthropic conference in San Francisco, I was invited to an event at the home of the founder's daughter,
Suzanne Dryan Felso. I immediately found Suzanne and
her mother, Mem Bernstein, to be incredibly grounded,
family-focused, and generous. It was there that I learned
about the opportunities and perils of a spend-down
approach. On one side of the coin is the ability to create
greater impact by minimizing the 'perpetual bureaucra-
cy' that can be an inevitable by-product of any large
foundation. On the other side, however, is the challenge
of defining a date for closing down what has hopefully
become a highly effective philanthropic team. People lose
their jobs, and the organizations that have come to rely on
the foundation's grants lose their funding—all at the stroke
of midnight.

Is the benefit worth the cost? It's a question that should be considered carefully. AVI CHAI offers a thoughtful look at this challenge in its 2014 and 2018 Annual Reports, both of which are available on its website at avichai.org.

■ Dynasty Philanthropy

Ask many families with wealth what they hope to achieve, and you'll likely hear the same answer over and over again: to create a family legacy. For families that have a history of giving, that almost always translates into supporting causes that reflect their multi-generational ideals. When older generations serve as philanthropic examples, giving often becomes part of the family DNA. It not only becomes an understood responsibility of every generation that follows, but for dynasty philanthropists, giving is part of their self-concept. It's simply who they are. Dynastic giving power takes many different forms. One of the most common forms—and often the most effective—is a family foundation. Warren Buffett's three children control four family foundations, to which he has given billions of dollars. I serve on the Board of the Isidore C and Penny Myers Foundation that is run by their heirs and gives $1 million every year to causes hand-picked by the founders. Dynasty philanthropy doesn't require Buffett-scale wealth. Family foundations typically make sense for families with $250,000 or more to dedicate to giving annually.

---

*See Chapter 4 for more on the opportunities
of family foundations.*

What kind of giving fits *you*? Regardless of how much wealth you have today—or how you've achieved it—it's important to think carefully about *why* you want to give, and then *how* you want to give. Keep in mind that while these are the most common categories of philanthropists, giving, by its nature, can't be boxed. As a 21ˢᵗ century philanthropist, you have the freedom to choose your path ahead. Money alone won't make you happy, but giving it away might!

The Power of Anonymous Giving

"At the end it's not about what you have
or even what you've accomplished.
It's about who you've lifted up,
who you've made better.
It's about what you've given back."
— *Denzel Washington*

While it doesn't quite fit as a 'type' of philanthropy, anonymous giving is an interesting form of giving for many reasons.

Maimonides, the medieval Sephardic Jewish philosopher, was perhaps the first to dive into the idea that giving has different levels—and that the highest level is when the donor remains completely anonymous. Even the rapper Jay-Z has weighed in on the subject in his song *Nickels and Dimes* with the line, "The greatest form of giving is anonymous to anonymous."

There are as many reasons to choose to give anonymously as there are anonymous givers. If you've ever made a political donation, you have seen the wave of requests that is spurred by even a small donation. Imagine the wave that hits when you've given a substantial amount to a public cause! For generous donors, remaining anonymous can be a powerful protector of their privacy.

One person might choose to give anonymously because they don't want the recipient to feel any weight of obligation for the gift. Another might feel their donation is outside the social norm—among their circle of friends, within their community, or among their family. Regardless of the reason, anonymous giving is a choice to consider.

'Curb Your Enthusiasm' gets anonymous

The topic of anonymous giving took the spotlight in an episode of the Emmy-winning show *Curb Your Enthusiasm*. In 'The Anonymous Donor' (Season 6, Episode 2), Larry David is being honored for donating a museum wing. To his dismay, he discovers that Ted Danson has also donated a wing, but anonymously. Ted, however, is anything but anonymous about his gift, happily sharing his secret with anyone who will listen— while insisting that he donated anonymously because he "doesn't want the fanfare."

Instead of celebrating Larry, the attention is turned to Ted as everyone (including California

Senator Barbara Boxer) praises him for donating anonymously. At his wit's end, Larry yells out, "No one told me I could be anonymous and tell people!"

The lesson learned? Giving anonymously can be done for many reasons. There are no rules! Whether you choose to be named or not is a personal choice. (Though if, like Larry and Ted, you do want to be recognized for your gift, giving anonymously is probably not the right choice for you!)

Denzel Washington is among many generous donors who choose to give anonymously—sometimes. He was an anonymous benefactor to the late Chadwick Boseman (of Black Panther fame), paying for Boseman's tuition at the British American Drama Academy's Midsummer in Oxford program when the young actor had declined to attend the prestigious training program due to a lack of funds. Boseman shared the heartwarming story when Washington received a Lifetime Achievement Award for the American Film Institute.

Years later, no one was surprised when the story emerged that Washington, overcome with emotion after visiting wounded troops, immediately took out his checkbook to make a large, on-the-spot donation for a new building at the Fisher House Foundation near Washington, D.C. (The actual story wasn't quite so theatrical; there was no checkbook in hand and no ink flying, but the donation itself was very real.) But while Washington does have a history of anonymous giving, the actor also gives publicly to many charities and foundations, including the Nelson Mandela Children's Fund, the Boys' and Girls' Clubs of America, the Elton John AIDS Foundation, and many more. For him, there are times he wishes to remain anonymous, and times he doesn't.

Again, the choice is personal, and there are no rules but your own.

Fame isn't required either. Near my home, there is a family that has been discreetly packing lunches and delivering them to local day laborers who wait at a well-known site in hopes of a job. Many of these men return to the spot day after day with no luck. The work this family does to purchase and pack meals for these men has an important impact on the community—and the giving is done completely anonymously.

Despite the reverence that's often given to anonymous givers, giving without being recognized isn't right for everyone.

Victor Klein, a dedicated philanthropist whom I got to know when we volunteered together at the Jewish Federation of Orange County (JFOC), was one of the most active volunteers I've met, supporting a wide variety of organizations with his time and money. In addition to the JFOC, he supported the Orange County Museum of Art; Heritage Pointe, a Jewish home for the aging in Mission Viejo, CA; and the University Synagogue in Irvine, CA, which he co-founded. Years ago, Victor and I were chatting about styles of philanthropy, and he explained to me why he didn't choose to give anonymously. "I want my name up on the walls of the synagogue," he told me. "I want it there for my grandchildren to see. I want to inspire them to continue to give long after I'm gone." When he died suddenly while on a bike ride at age 83, I thought of his words and his wisdom. For him, being named mattered, and for all the right reasons. For you, being named may be the key to inspiring others—from your family to complete strangers—to follow in your footsteps.

EXERCISE:

What are your motivations and values?

Articulating your motivations and values can help you to develop a proactive and effective giving strategy. This can help you direct your time, money, and resources toward the people and causes that matter most to you rather than giving reactively to funding requests. Ultimately, your motivations and values provide the anchor for decision-making at each step of the philanthropy process.

The following two exercises are designed to be completed together.

Activity A—Reflect on Your Motivation & Values provides reflection questions to help clarify the motivations driving your giving, as well as the values underlying it.

Activity B—Select Your Values helps you identify values that are important to you to help guide your giving strategy.

A
REFLECT ON YOUR MOTIVATIONS & VALUES

Instructions

Review the questions in Activity A to clarify your philanthropic motivations and identify the values important to your giving. Write down your thoughts, taking time to consider each question fully.

What motivates you to give?

_____

_____

_____

_____

What do you want to change in the world?

_____

_____

_____

_____

_____

What life experiences have shaped your desire to give your time or money?

_____

_____

_____

_____

_____

What do you want to sustain or keep the same in the world?

_____

_____

_____

_____

_____

What values are important to your giving?

_____

_____

_____

_____

Where have you given your time and money in the
past—and why?

_____

_____

_____

_____

_____

Where do you give your time and money currently—
and why?

_____

_____

_____

_____

What issues interest you most—and why?

_____

_____

_____

_____

What issues feel most pressing to you—and why?

_____

_____

_____

_____

What life experiences have shaped you, the way you
look at the world, and your approach to giving?

_____

_____

_____

_____

What are some moments or experiences in which
you felt like you had some impact on the world?

_____

_____

_____

_____

_____

B
SELECT YOUR VALUES

Instructions: Part 1

Use the following list to reflect on which values are important to you. You may also write in additional values. For couples and families, you can choose to do this activity together. It can also be helpful to do this activity individually, and then share your responses and discuss areas of overlap and differences.

ACCESSIBILITY	EFFECTIVENESS
ACCOUNTABILITY	EMPATHY
AUTHENTICITY	EMPOWERMENT
COLLABORATION	EQUITY
COMMUNITY	EXPLORATION
CONNECTION	FAIRNESS
COURAGE	FAITH
CREATIVITY	FAMILY
CURIOSITY	FREEDOM
DIGNITY	FUN
DISCIPLINE	GENEROSITY
DIVERSITY	GROWTH

HAPPINESS	PATRIOTISM
HARMONY	PEACE
HEALTH	PERSISTENCE
HONOR	RESOURCEFULNESS
HUMILITY	RESPECT
HUMOR	SECURITY
INDEPENDENCE	SELF-ACTUALIZATION
INNOVATION	SERVICE
INTEGRITY	SIMPLICITY
INTERDEPENDENCE	SPIRITUALITY
JOY	SPONTANEITY
JUSTICE	STEWARDSHIP
KINDNESS	TRADITION
LEADERSHIP	TRUSTWORTHINESS
LOVE	UNITY
LOYALTY	WELLBEING
PASSION	

Instructions: Part 2

Write in the five values that resonate the most with you. These are your core values.

1:_____

2:_____

3:_____

4:_____

5:_____

Now, reflect on how each of these five values might influence your charitable planning and giving decisions.

_____

_____

_____

_____

_____

_____

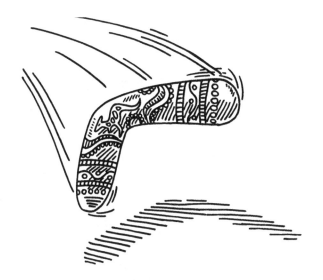

CHAPTER 2

The Personal Side of Giving

"If you want something, give it."
— *Deepak Chopra*

Giving can have a big impact... for a large group of people, a cause, or a cure.

At other times, giving can have a small impact... sometimes for just one person.

But in every case I know of, the act of giving begins an unseen chain reaction that creates wave upon wave of positive change.

And one of those waves of change occurs within the giver. Like a boomerang.

Giving creates one of life's great circles. The more we give away, the more we receive.

How Giving Can Help Fulfill Your Life

"In the end generosity is the best way
of becoming more, more, and more joyful."
— *Desmond Tutu*

It's a simple fact: giving rewards both the giver and the receiver.

We've already explored the emotional and, to some extent, the physical rewards of giving, but research shows that giving has some very practical benefits as well.

While he was attending the University of Pennsylvania, our son Blaze introduced me to the work of Adam Grant, an organizational psychologist, author, and the highest-rated professor at the Wharton School. Grant's 2013 book, *Give and Take: A Revolutionary Approach to Success,* looks at how "an attitude of extreme giving at work" often results in exponential benefits for the giver.

In his research, Grant found three basic kinds of people that exist in every workplace: givers, takers, and matchers. (In my own experience, I can guess that these categories reach far beyond the confines of the office!) 'Givers' help others and work to create success for the group 'Matchers' strive for fair and equal exchanges—a sort of tit-for-tat mentality. 'Takers' focus on what they can get from others. They adhere to the idea that, in the words of basketball great Michael Jordan, "to be successful, you have to be selfish."

Any dedicated giver will be overjoyed to learn that Grant's work shows that, ultimately, Takers don't win the game (sorry Michael). One obvious reason for this is that Takers lose the respect of others because their actions damage their reputations. After all, who would choose to have a Taker on their team? But the reason Givers are typically more successful than their selfish colleagues isn't rooted in the *lack* of success of Takers. On the contrary, Grant's research revealed that because Givers are known to make decisions based on what's 'good for the team,' they help everyone rise up. They rise to top positions in the workplace and society because they are known for focusing on the greater good. And because they make it a habit to help others, their large networks of appreciative friends and colleagues are often more than happy to help when Givers ask for assistance. Givers also have a positive influence, often increasing the level of giving by those around them. That's peer pressure at its best!

I've witnessed this myself in my own office, where I'm fortunate to be surrounded by a wonderful team of Givers. There is not a selfish Taker in the group, and it shows in everything we do. By consistently helping each other excel, we have achieved remarkable professional success, but we also work as Givers in a charitable sense, sharing the responsibility for choosing which organizations to support each year. Recent recipients of our efforts have included the National Urban League (nul.org), World Central Kitchen (wck.org), and the National Multiple Sclerosis Society (nationalmssociety.org). The environment we've been able to create is unique in that it is built solidly on the concept of giving.

At University of Pennsylvania, Grant showed that Givers are rewarded in the workplace. Other studies have shown that those rewards reach into our personal lives as well.

A study by Michael Norton and his colleagues at Harvard Business School demonstrated that people are happier when they spend money on others than when they spend on themselves. As part of the study, 632 American men and women were asked how much their salary was, how much they spent each month on household expenses and gifts for themselves, and how much they gave to others in the form of donations to charities. They were then asked to rate their level of happiness. The survey results were clear: regardless of the level of income or expenses, people who gave more to others—the Givers—rated themselves happier than people who spent mostly on themselves.

The science behind the 'ripple effect' of giving

Public acts of giving create a ripple effect—a wave of generosity that can influence others to give as well. Adam Grant talks about this effect as the 'positive influence' that givers have on others. Science tells us that this influence is created by more than just a desire to do good.

Lab studies conducted by Paul Zak, the founder of the Center for Neuroeconomics Studies at Claremont Graduate University, found that the brain released the hormone oxytocin when participants shared and experienced gratitude.[4] In a separate study[5], Zak and his team found that oxytocin increases generosity in people.

Most mothers are very aware of the effect of oxytocin when breastfeeding a newborn baby. This powerful hormone is responsible for the physical release of breast milk so the mother can feed her baby, but it also fosters feelings of love and nurturing, and it helps form a strong emotional bond between mother and child. Zak's study shows us that oxytocin plays an important role in the wider world—especially when it comes to giving.

---

[4] "Empathy toward strangers triggers oxytocin release and subsequent generosity," Jorge Barraza and Paul Zak, National Library of Medicine, June 2009.
[5] "Oxytocin Increases Generosity in Humans," Paul J. Zak, Angela A. Stanton, and Sheila Ahmadi, PMC US National Library of Medicine National Institutes of Health, November 2007.

Giving After Suffering a Loss

"You've been so kind and generous
I don't know how you keep on giving"
— *Natalie Merchant*

Science may help us understand how giving helps fulfill our lives, but no survey or lab study or scientific model can reveal what each of us feels on the inside. For me, my experiences—and what I experience each time I give—is the most important 'proof' that I am truly fulfilled through the act of giving.

Just after New Year's Day in 2018, my son Blaze died at just 19 years old. My wife Jeanne and I found ourselves desperately searching for meaning. We were a close family, and suddenly a big piece of who we were had disappeared. What we soon learned was that not only did giving to others feel good in the days and weeks following Blaze's death, but that giving would continue to heal us in the months and years to come.

As a family, philanthropy had always been a way of life for us. We financially supported causes and organizations that mattered to us, and we encouraged our kids to be active philanthropists in their own ways, giving time and resources to help make a difference. Our daughter Beaue found a passion for giving as a member of the Young Philanthropists, a teen program at the Jewish Community Center of Orange County. Jay worked with us at Second Harvest Food Bank. Blaze became a bona fide community activist at University of Pennsylvania, taking direct action to push for improvements in on-campus safety and other policy reforms. In a classic example of the 'ripple effect' of giving, everything we gave as a family came back to us when we needed help ourselves. In time, we were able to continue the cycle of giving once again.

In the months after Blaze died, Jeanne and I were still fragile and trying to find our footing again. Right after our son's funeral, a family we knew performed a quiet act of giving: they passed along the key to their family vacation home in Laguna Beach with the message that we could use it whenever we needed a place to retreat. That simple gift (large by our standards) became a much needed godsend. Over the next few months, we would go there to get away from the stress, the memories, and the anger. It was our way to escape and get out of our own heads.

One of my daily routines when we were there was to walk to a tiny café nearby for one of my favorite morning treats: a cup of Vietnamese coffee with oat milk. One morning, as I sleepily waited for the barista to prepare my order, I saw a young homeless man go into the bathroom. When he came out, he stood for a moment to stare at the baked goods under glass before walking back outside where he sat down on the sidewalk, empty handed. He clearly needed help, so I ordered a second coffee and a pastry and sat down next to him to share a small meal. As we ate together and chatted, he told me his story. He had come from Philadelphia (where Blaze had been at school), following a girl to

California. Soon after he arrived, the relationship ended. Now he was alone, out of work, homeless, and miserable.

Almost immediately after Blaze's death, Jeanne and I started a Donor Advised Fund in his memory, the Blaze Bernstein Memorial Fund. We also created the #BlazeItForward campaign to encourage others to take action to promote kindness, love, empathy, and respect. As part of the campaign, we had business-sized cards made to hand out with any act of kindness. The goal: to create a continuous cycle of giving that honored Blaze.

To learn about Donor Advised Funds (DAFs),
see Chapter 4.

After chatting with this young man for quite a while, I handed him a #BlazeItForward card with a $100 bill, and I asked him to pay it forward. "Buy what you need, but also share it with someone else who needs help." He looked at me, stunned. In my view, what I'd given was generous, but it was certainly no sacrifice. I just wanted to help. For him, that $100 was a precious gift. "You have no idea how this changes things for me," he told me. "I can actually live like a normal human being without begging to eat for the next three or four days." I had made a difference in a way I could never have imagined… and yes, it felt amazing.

Not all acts of giving are so dramatic, but even the smallest acts can be fulfilling.

When Blaze's birthday came that first year after his death, I knew the only way I could cope was to spend the day giving to others. As a volunteer at the Orangewood Foundation in Santa Ana, California, I was very familiar with the work they do to help foster youth, many of whom are homeless. So to celebrate Blaze in my own way, I took dessert and homemade cookies to share. At a time when I felt so helpless, that small act of giving gave me a new perspective—and it lifted me up.

According to science (and according to me!) giving helps the recipient and fulfills the giver. It's one of the greatest benefits of becoming a modern philanthropist.

Giving and the Ultra Wealthy

"If you're in the luckiest one percent of humanity,
you owe it to the rest of humanity
to think about the other 99 percent."
— *Warren Buffett*

Today's billionaires have a whole new look—and they are creating a new kind of personal impact.

According to research firm Wealth-X, today's ultra-wealthy donors are more personally involved than ever. Rather than taking the traditional approach of supporting large, established organizations, they are taking the time to hand pick which organizations to support and to investigate where every dollar is spent. They are also giving an unprecedented amount of their own time and skills. Instead of financing buildings (with their names boldly emblazoned at the top), they are filling seats on nonprofit boards, volunteering in person, and getting involved at the ground level. This trend of philanthropic 'co-creation' demands far greater oversight into where and how funds are distributed, and it is driving a massive shift in the types of organizations that are supported by charitable giving.

The results have been tremendous.

Perhaps the most obvious result of this desire to create personal impact is the trend toward focusing on a single cause rather than spreading giving over a wide variety of causes. This laser focus enables the ultra-wealthy to achieve a stunning level of impact. For instance:

- The Gates Foundation, the world's wealthiest charitable foundation, has contributed more than $2.9 billion in grants to combat malaria in Africa—an effort that has helped save thousands of lives and create a healthier world for future generations.

- The Walton Family Foundation, established by Walmart founder Sam Walton, is now controlled by Walton's four children. They recently fine-tuned their giving to focus on three areas: improving K-12 education, protecting rivers and oceans, and supporting economic-development projects in their home state of Arkansas. The foundation has committed to giving $2.2 billion to support these causes in the next five years, with $1 billion going to education alone.

- Brian Armstrong is the co-founder and CEO of Coinbase, a crypto-currency trading app. At 35 years old, he has already joined the ranks of today's ultra-wealthy givers. He created GiveCrypto.org, an evergreen endowment fund that uses cryptocurrency to empower people living in poverty around the globe. As of 2020, the fund has raised more than $4 million and distributed it via direct cash transfers to those in need.

■ Tony Hawk, or "Birdman," earned his fame as a professional skate-
boarder and the pioneer of modern vertical skateboarding. He later
earned his financial fortune as an entrepreneur and the owner of the
skateboard company Birdhouse. In response to the lack of safe, legal
places to skate in America, he established the Tony Hawk Foundation in 2002. Since then, the foundation has awarded over $10 mil-
lion to more than 600 public skatepark projects in all 50 US states,
as well as $150,000 to support the Skateistan program in Afghani-
stan, Cambodia, and Africa. The organization changed its name to
The Skatepark Project in 2020.

'Impact philanthropy' has quickly become a big buzzword among ultra-wealthy givers. While the idea is rooted in the quest to create social
impact by improving the lives of others, it also relies on identifying
problems and developing solutions, exploring where donors can find
the best 'bang for the buck,' and continuously refining giving strategies
to make the greatest possible difference.

It's not just the approach to giving that has changed. The people that
comprise today's ultra-wealthy philanthropists are also dramatically
different than in past generations. Rather than inheriting wealth, many
of today's billionaires grew up far from the lap of luxury, and their approach to giving reflects their less privileged beginnings.

The newly wealthy are inspired to give back

"I love when people say you come from 'humble beginnings'... [it] means you were poor as hell."
— *Tyler Perry*

In September 2020, Forbes named filmmaker Tyler Perry "Hollywood's Newest Billionaire." Once homeless and a high school dropout, Perry's wealth includes income from his popular Madea movies and his Tyler Perry Studios (now the largest film production studio in the US), as well as his $60 million stake in BET+. Perry has financed dozens of productions from Black creators. He has also donated $1 million to the NAACP in honor of the organization's centennial, $1 million to help Haiti earthquake survivors rebuild, and another $1 million to help victims of Hurricane Harvey. In 2020, he announced construction of a compound for trafficked women, homeless women, and LGBTQ youth. Since 2006, his charitable organization, The Perry Foundation, has aimed to transform tragedy into triumph by seeding individual potential, supporting communities, and harvesting sustainable change.

"Something greater rises up every time we give."
— Jeff Bezos

When Amazon founder Jeff Bezos, one of the richest individuals in the world, was born, his mother was a 17-year old high school student and his father owned a bike shop. In high school, he worked as a short-order line cook. Bezos and his ex-wife, MacKenzie Scott, gave an estimated $2 billion in 2018 to fund nonprofit schools and homeless charities through their Day One Fund.

"Let's make philanthropy a value, a faith, a commitment, and a lifestyle."
— Dong Fangjun

Dong Fangjun, chairman of the Chinese investment firm Dongfang Huiquan Financial Holdings, was born in a remote village in China to a poor family of farmers. At age 27, he became disabled in a serious car accident. He founded the Dongfangjun Charity Foundation which focuses on caring for veterans, disaster relief, poverty alleviation, reviving traditional culture, supporting education, and building a harmonious society.

> "Assists is what Earvin is all about.
> That's what my whole life has been,
> assisting others."
> — *Magic Johnson*

Earvin 'Magic' Johnson grew up in Lansing, Michigan, where his mother worked as a GM assembly line worker and his father worked as a janitor. Considered one of the greatest basketball players in NBA history, his long career with the LA Lakers ended abruptly in 1991 when he announced his retirement after testing positive for HIV, the virus that causes AIDS. That year, he started the Magic Johnson Foundation that has since raised more than $20 million to help prevent the spread of HIV/AIDS through education and awareness. His company, Magic Johnson Enterprises, invests in movie theaters, fitness centers, and restaurants in low-income neighborhoods across the US.

These are far from the only examples. Facebook founder Mark Zuckerberg's father was a dentist, and his mother was a psychologist. After earning his fortune as an internet tycoon, he created a multibillion-dollar charity with his wife, Priscilla Chan. Oprah Winfrey's life began in poverty. She went on to build a billion-dollar media empire and create multiple charitable foundations. Stephen Schwarzman grew up watching his father run a dry-goods store in Philadelphia and rose to become chairman and CEO of The Blackstone Group. In 2018, he gave $350 million to establish MIT Schwarzman College of Computing—just one of his many generous gifts focused on education. These billionaires and many others are changing how the world sees philanthropy. And they are changing the shape of philanthropy itself.

The Giving Pledge is one more example of this morphing of philanthropy as we know it.

The brainchild of Bill and Melinda French Gates and Warren Buffett, The Giving Pledge began in August 2010 when 40 of America's wealthiest people each committed to donating the majority of their wealth to address some of society's most pressing problems, either within their lifetimes or immediately after their death. But

The Giving Pledge

the Pledge is much more than just a one-time financial commitment. Givers who make the pledge are welcomed into an energized community that includes some of the world's most engaged philanthropists. Together, they discuss challenges, share successes and failures, and explore new ideas related to wise giving strategies. Their goal: to set a new standard of public accountability for generosity.

In 2013, the pledge went global, adding signatories from Australia, Germany, India, Malaysia, Russia, South Africa, Ukraine, and the United Kingdom. By 2020, more than 200 of the world's wealthiest individuals, couples, and families had made the pledge, including people of every generation—from as young as 30 to as old as their upper 90s—living in 24 countries around the world.

Unlike a traditional foundation or pooled fund, the Giving Pledge provides no oversight or distribution of donations in any form.

Members commit publicly to the pledge. They list themselves on GivingPledge.org and meet annually to share ideas and learn from each other's experiences. This unique approach sets the stage for a different sort of philanthropic path that focuses on fostering commitment, community, and personal passion.

If your good fortune has placed you among the ultra-wealthy, you have achieved a level of wealth far beyond most people's hopes and dreams. Now is the time to use a portion of that wealth to create an impact that matters to you and to become an 'ultra-giver.'

Now is the time to act.

_____

To learn about a Giving Pledge for 'the other 99%'
see Chapter 5.

_____

Anyone Can Make a Difference

"No one has ever become poor by giving."
— Anne Frank

The ultra-wealthy may be reshaping how we see philanthropy in the world, but having an impact on the world doesn't require that you be ultra wealthy… or even well off. Rich, not so rich, or far from rich, anyone can make a difference. The only prerequisite for giving is a desire to help others.

To illustrate the fact that anyone can be a philanthropist, the Lilly Family School of Philanthropy at Indiana University joined forces with the YWCA and Facebook to spotlight the stories of real-world philanthropists—women who have donated their "time, treasure, talent, and testimony" to make the world a better place. The campaign includes a series of personal stories that are posted to social media, and it encourages others to post their own stories using the hashtag #IAmAPhilan-thropist. The result has been a growing forum of stories, examples, and inspiration from women of all ages, races, and income levels who are giving what they can to make a difference.

Happily, today's online world makes it easier than ever to give any amount you choose, and to research and select the people and causes you want to support.

- **Facebook Fundraisers** enable any Facebook user to request do-nations for charitable and other causes. The program is free to use, and pages and donate buttons are easy to create. Donations are paid directly to the non-profit, or the money can be distributed through Donor Advised Funds like Network or the PayPal Giving Fund.

- **The AmazonSmile program** allows shoppers to select from over a million eligible charitable organizations, to which Amazon then donates 0.5% of the user's eligible purchases. Once a charity is cho-sen, shoppers simply enter the Amazon site using the smile.amazon.com URL rather than amazon.com.

- **Corporate matching programs** are offered by 65% of large US companies and many smaller organizations to help employees boost their giving power. The Google Matching Gifts program matches its employee donations to non-profit organizations. American Express works with GlobalGiving to provide its employees with a gift-match-ing program. Disney matches donations for full-time and part-time employees for gifts of up to $15,000 and has a VoluntEARS program that offers volunteer grants to employees who offer time (rather than money) to nonprofits. Other companies with fantastic matching programs include Starbucks, Apple, GE, and Boeing.

---

*To learn about the power of Corporate
Matching Programs, see Chapter 4.*

Of course, money may make giving easy, but it isn't the only way to make a donation. If you have household items, clothing, books, or other items to donate, the options for where to donate are vast. Through eBay's Giving Works program, you can auction off items and donate a percentage of the final sale to your charity of choice once they are sold. Habitat for Humanity Restore accepts donations of all sorts of household items at its donation centers—or it will schedule a pickup of large items at no charge. Baby2Baby happily accepts gently used baby gear (clothing, backpacks, diapers, beds, blankets, toys, car seats, and more) to distribute to shelters and children's hospitals. Local food banks accept non-perishable foods, and Move for Hunger will even pick up unwanted food and deliver it to food banks in 50 US states and Canada. Other nationwide organizations include Goodwill, Salvation Army, and Pickup Please, which is run by the Vietnam Veterans of America.

Giving your time to help others makes giving deeply personal. During the pandemic, widespread one-to-one giving was a silver lining for an otherwise dire situation. According to IUPUI, 48% of US households engaged in some form of giving in response to the pandemic[6]—some in very unconventional ways. In addition to buying gift cards to support local restaurants and continuing to pay household employees such as housekeepers, childcare providers, and gardeners, many people found ways to give their time. Younger people volunteered to shop for

---

[6] "Giving in the pandemic: More than half of Americans have found ways to help those hit by COVID-19 hardship," by Tessa Skidmore, Women's Philanthropy Institute, Indiana University.

groceries. It seemed anyone with a sewing machine was sewing masks and donating them to medical professionals or to people in their communities. Every one of these activities made a difference. Hopefully, this sort of personal, one-to-one giving will continue now that people seem to have rediscovered the joys of giving to others.

Low-income kids choose giving over receiving

At the Boys and Girls Club of Metro Atlanta, a few dozen kids ages 6 to 11 years old were asked what they wanted for Christmas, as well as what they thought their mom or dad wanted for Christmas. They were told they would receive a gift, but there was a catch: they had to choose between a gift for themselves or a gift for one of their parents.

On their own wish lists were all things you might expect: a Barbie house. An Xbox 360. A trophy case. A computer. And though they were clearly excited about these things, in the video that shows their reactions, their faces light up when they talk about what their parents might like. A television. A watch. A ring (because "my mom's never really had a ring").

In the true spirit of giving, each of them chose the gift for their mom or dad. When asked why, their answers were simple:

"I get gifts every year from my family, and my mom never gets anything."

"Because legos don't really matter. Your family matters."

"Now I have the opportunity to give my dad something."

These kids, who come from an area where 83% of families live in poverty, chose to put their parents' happiness first. Even though they have so little, they showed that they care more about giving than receiving.

Of course, as the old saying goes, *time is money*. And when it comes to giving, offering what you *can* give is what matters most. It doesn't matter whether you are giving your time, treasure, talent, or testimony—as long as you are giving something to help others.

EXERCISE:

The simple joy of one-to-one giving

Anyone reading a book on giving is probably already a giver. Maybe you donate to a handful of charities. Perhaps you give regularly to your place of worship. And yet many active philanthropists haven't experienced the simple joy of one-to-one giving.

To give you new insights into how you can experience the personal side of giving, complete the following activities in a single day, taking time to reflect on your experience as soon as possible after the activity is finished.

Activity C—#BlazeitForward explores the power of one-to-one giving in the real world.

Activity D—Reflection invites you to look closely at your motivation for giving and how to translate your experience into your long-term giving strategy.

C
#BlazeitForward

. . . .

Instructions

When you are going about your day, choose a way to pay for a stranger's meal or coffee. Keep it simple and, if possible, make it anonymous.

Write down what you gave, how you chose the recipient of your gift, and your immediate feelings about the experience.

_____

_____

_____

_____

_____

_____

_____

_____

_____

_____

D
REFLECT ON YOUR GIVING EXPERIENCE

Instructions

Now take a deeper look at your experience with one-to-one giving and how it might influence how you choose to give in the future. Answer each of the questions below:

What motivated you to give in the manner you did?

_____

_____

_____

_____

_____

Did the dollar amount of the gift impact how you felt about the experience?

_____

_____

_____

_____

_____

If you were able to give anonymously, did that shift the experience at all?

_____

_____

_____

_____

_____

_____

_____

How could you expand on this type of giving on a regular basis?

_____

_____

_____

_____

_____

_____

_____

_____

_____

If you gave in this way again, would you change how you gave?

_____

_____

_____

_____

_____

Did you sense any sort of chain reaction or 'ripple effect' from giving?

_____

_____

_____

_____

How did this act of giving change your view of yourself? Of the recipient? Of the people around you?

_____

_____

_____

_____

_____

CHAPTER 3

Barriers to Giving

"I can't give everything,
I can't give everything away,
I can't give everything away."
— David Bowie

'I Can't Give Everything Away'
(from his posthumous album 'Blackstar,' 2016)

If you see someone hungry on the street, do you stop to help?

If you see a need for change in the world, do you take action?

If you're given the choice between giving to yourself and giving to others, what is your first instinct?

In the real world, giving can be a challenge. So many things can keep us from taking action—large or small.

Overcoming these barriers allows us to create greater impact. And it's easier than you may think.

The Paradox of Giving

"Give it away, give it away, give it away, now!"
— *Red Hot Chili Peppers, 'Give it Away'*

Not long ago, a friend invited me to spend the day on his new boat. I had no idea what to expect. I knew he and his family owned a very successful business, but I also knew that he was extremely practical with his money, rarely splurging on even small luxuries. But a boat? I was surprised… and intrigued.

When I arrived at the dock, I was stunned. This was no small extravagance. It was pure opulence. I'm no expert, but I would guess my friend's new toy cost as much as a small house here in Southern California. Sure, he owned the boat with his family, but it still didn't mesh with the person I had come to know over the years. What had changed? What had caused my friend's practical nature to flip upside down, seemingly overnight?

Once we were out on the water, my questions were answered. He told me he'd recently received a serious health diagnosis. It had been a wakeup call of sorts. For years, he had been the poster child for frugality. Now, he wanted to enjoy his material wealth to the fullest while he still could. The boat was just one of the many lavish purchases on his list. He told me his goal was to "enjoy every minute… even if it means spending every dollar."

Facing his own mortality was a game changer.

As Mark Manson states so well in his #1 *New York Times* Bestseller, *The Subtle Art of Not Giving a F*ck: A Counterintuitive Approach to Living a Good Life*, "while money is nice, caring about what you do with your life is better, because true wealth is about experience." At 60 years old, my friend had gotten a crash course in life, and his first step forward consisted of finding new ways to live it well.

My mind immediately went to another method of finding fulfillment: giving. And I didn't keep my thoughts to myself. The more my friend and I chatted, the more I elaborated on the whole idea of philanthropy… about how it had changed my own life, and how I had seen it change the lives of people of all ages and all levels of wealth. His ears perked up immediately; I had his attention. By the time we arrived back at the dock, he asked if we could schedule a time to talk more about how he could begin creating his own philanthropic strategy.

What was holding him back before? I truly believe that giving his money away simply hadn't occurred to him.

---

*Ready to start creating your own strategy for giving?
See Chapter 4 to learn how.*

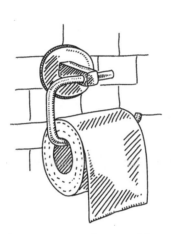

The Scarcity Effect

"Helping people doesn't have to be
an unsound financial strategy."
— *Melinda French Gates*

Of course, not everyone has such an abundance of resources. For my friend with the boat, it's quite easy to enjoy his wealth and share a portion of his resources with others. For others, the idea of becoming a philanthropist can come with a large dose of fear. What if I give too much today and can't support myself and my family tomorrow? What if my financial reality shifts and my own resources become scarce? What if the stock market crashes? What if I get sick?

What if the unthinkable happens—like a global pandemic that puts the entire economy on hold for months or years at a time?

Anyone who doubted the potential for change and scarcity certainly got a major wakeup call during the pandemic. When toilet paper can't be found, the idea of scarcity suddenly becomes all too real! But the fear of scarcity doesn't have to hold us back from giving.

I've talked about giving strategies for people with fewer resources. If your financial resources are limited, you can still be a philanthropist by giving freely of your time and talent to help others, without sacrificing your financial resources. On the other hand, if you *do* have more than enough to share, but the fear of scarcity is holding you back, there are steps you can take to become a generous donor—with absolutely no risk of depleting your own resources while you still need them.

Just look at Isidore Myers. A WWII Veteran and successful entrepreneur, 'Izzy' accumulated an abundance of resources in his lifetime—but they hadn't come easily. The son of Polish immigrants, he grew up in Akron, Ohio, where he began helping to support his family by selling newspapers on the street when he was just 6 years old. He knew what struggle felt like, and he never wanted his children or grandchildren to experience the same challenges.

After achieving great financial success in industrial real estate, Izzy's focus changed to giving back. Beginning in the early 1990s, Izzy spent most of his time worrying about how to give his money away. The catch: he didn't want to give it away until he died. And because he had a gift for managing his money, he felt he could maximize the impact of his gifts by growing his wealth while he lived, and then give it all away afterwards.

To bring that goal to life, he and his wife Penny established a charitable organization, the Isidore C and Penny W Myers Foundation. Designed to support the causes with which the couple had a personal and emotional connection, the foundation focused on giving to educational, religious, medical, and social welfare organizations. Izzy passed away peacefully in 2013 at the impressive age of 96. The foundation continues to give generously to a variety of charities every year.

Izzy made the choice to give, but to him, waiting until after his death made perfect sense.

No matter how many or how few resources you have today, the fear of scarcity can be very real. You should never give while you are living because you feel you 'should.' But that fear doesn't mean you can't be a generous philanthropist. If you're not sure whether giving during your lifetime or afterwards is best for you, ask for advice from a trusted financial advisor and make the right personal choice based on the facts.

The Bystander Effect

"Don't be the bystander. Be the hero."
— *Anonymous*

Imagine this scenario: You're in a crowded restaurant when another diner begins to cough loudly. Suddenly his wife starts yelling for help as he grasps frantically at his throat. With every second, the fact that he's choking becomes more obvious, but no one moves to help. Surely at least one person here knows the Heimlich Maneuver? You search your memory for what you learned in that CPR class years ago, hoping you can still recall enough to help. One fact you remember clearly: it only takes four to six minutes of no oxygen to cause serious damage to the brain. Ten more seconds go by, and still no one comes to his aid.

You have to do something. It's now or never.

If you've ever been in an urgent situation like this, you know just how scary it can be. And you know how a crowd will freeze and watch and wait—even when facing life or death. Why don't more people act? The answer is rooted in what social psychologists call the 'bystander effect.'

Their research has found that people are less likely to offer help when they are in a group than when they are alone. In other words, if they think someone else might help, they choose to step back and remain a bystander rather than taking action themselves. Sadly, this effect too often means that *no one* comes to the rescue.

In his popular book *The Tipping Point,* Malcolm Gladwell discusses the power of the bystander effect, telling the well-known story of Kitty Genovese who was stabbed to death on the street in Queens in the 1960s. Though dozens of witnesses said they heard her cries for help, each person either assumed no actual crime was taking place—that this was just a lovers' quarrel—or that someone had already called the police. Thirty minutes later, the woman was dead.

In the world of philanthropy, the consequences of the bystander effect may not often be deadly, but they can certainly create devastation. The reason: help isn't provided when it is needed most.

CPR training teaches how to bypass the bystander effect

In an emergency, it's natural to yell out, "Call the police!" or "Someone call 911!" But an important part of CPR training instructs participants to be more specific. Instead of a general command, the approach that generates real results is to be very specific. Point directly at one person and say, "You! Call 911!"

It's crazy to think that most people will fail to act—even in a life-threatening situation—unless they are asked directly to do something specific. But the power of the bystander effect has been demonstrated over and over again, both in social psychology experiments (the work of social psychologists John Darley and Bibb Latané is particularly interesting) and in example after example in the world around us.

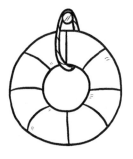

As philanthropists, it is vital that we find our own methods to bypass the bystander effect—for ourselves and for others—so help arrives before it's too late.

The bystander effect is rooted in the diffusion of responsibility. If others can help, you might think, why should I? But if not you, who?

Luckily, whether a small group of diners is watching someone choke, or the global community is watching a community suffer a natural disaster, witnessing a humanitarian crisis, or learning about the increasing rate of suicide during a pandemic, there are ways to stop the bystander effect in its tracks. Here are just three approaches that have been proven to drive results:

1. Make it personal.

Last Christmas, my friend Ashley was thrilled to see a special 'collaboration' shoe from TOMS˙. Not only was she already a fan of the company's approach to giving (TOMS donates $1 to charity for every $3 it makes), but this special release offered an extra perk for givers: a One for One® donation to St. Jude Children's Hospital. When she mentioned it to her husband, his response was less than enthusiastic. "You buying one pair of shoes isn't going to matter... it's just a drop in the bucket." In other words, "someone else will handle it." But for

76

Ashley, the cause was personal. When her 11-year-old cousin Danielle was diagnosed with a rare bone marrow disease called Diamond Blackfan Anemia (DFA), she had been a patient at St. Jude. Though Danielle died of the disease, Ashley was able to witness first-hand how important St. Jude's work was. Even though her budget was tight, she bought the shoes. "I feel great every time I wear them," she told me. "Maybe it wasn't much, but I'm happy knowing I helped make a difference."

2. Give it a face.

The *New York Times Neediest Cases Fund* has raised more than $300 million since it was established in 1911. While the fund supports "a global community of people less fortunate," including residents of New York and beyond, it is the up-close-and-personal profiles on those in need that have helped draw a huge wave of donations from people around the world. In 2020, many of the cases profiled were pandemic related. Families who lost loved ones to COVID-19 and were unable to pay rent. Workers forced into lockdown who needed computers to stay employed. Performing artists—musicians, actors, dancers, and more—who were suddenly and indefinitely unemployed. Essential workers who needed a hot meal. In each case, *The New York Times* put a face to the crisis, and seeing the real people who needed and received help encouraged people to give. The result: the 2020 campaign raised more than $3 million in the first 4 months alone.

3. Make it a movement.

Originally coined by social activist Tarana Burke in 2006, the term 'Me Too' became a global phenomenon in 2017 following the arrest of Hollywood mogul Harvey Weinstein for the sexual harassment and rape of dozens of women over a 20-year period. In the year that followed, the hashtag #MeToo was used more than 19 million times on

Twitter—more than 55,000 times *per day*. When the Time's Up Legal Defense Fund was created to assist victims of sexual harassment, abuse, or retaliation with legal assistance, the response was enthusiastic. The GoFundMe campaign raised more money than any other campaign in the platform's history: over $24 million in two years. The campaign stopped accepting GoFundMe donations in May 2019 when it was transitioned to a private foundation, but the movement continues to live on.

The bystander effect is only a barrier to giving if you let it. If you find yourself thinking, "surely, someone else will help," come back to the question, "If not me, who?" Find the issues that are personal... for *you*. Give them a face that matters... to *you*. And discover what causes matter enough to *you* to join the movement—or create one.

To learn how to turn your own moment of giving into a movement, see Chapter 5.

Never Enough

"Even the smallest person can change the course of the future."
— *J.R.R. Tolkien, The Fellowship of the Ring*

No gift is too small. It's that simple.

Almost every day, I drive by the local hospital. The name of its biggest donor is emblazoned on the side of the building. The same is true at the performing arts center across the courtyard from my office, at the art museum nearby, and even at the botanical garden. For anyone who isn't giving millions (which, let's be honest, is most of us), it can make your smaller gift seem insignificant. Like it's never enough. If I could shout it from the rooftops, I would: no gift is too small! And your gift *matters*.

If you doubt my words, this statistic may surprise you:

According to Nonprofits Course, the average one-time online donation to charity is just $128 dollars. The average annual donation to charity for recurring donors is $326. It may not sound like much, but those dollars add up! The total amount of online giving hit $31 *billion* in 2017, and Americans gave a total of $410 billion to charities in the same year. That level of giving has been increasing every year. In 2019, donations received on #GivingTuesday (the Tuesday after Thanksgiving which is dedicated to charitable giving) totaled almost $2 billion.[7] Donations on #GivingTuesday 2020 were up 25% compared to 2019, bringing in $2.5 billion in a single day.[8]

The average single gift: $134.

The 3 Dollar Challenge

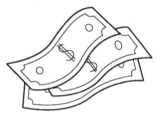

In the early days of COVID-19, Jack and Kate Adler, 19-year-old twins from Villanova, PA, wanted to find a way to raise funds to support coronavirus relief. With time on their hands during lockdown, they created a grassroots fundraising campaign called 'the 3 Dollar Challenge' (3DC) on Instagram.

Using Venmo and GoFundMe, they asked people to post a story on Instagram about something they couldn't wait to get back to after quarantine—and then donate $3 that would be equally divided among three different charities: Feed America, the CDC, and Direct Relief. In just 24 hours, the campaign raised over $10,000.

In November 2020, the Adlers announced a second campaign to support wellness and suicide prevention for college students amid the pandemic, with all funds bene-

---

[7] "GivingTuesday 2019 Brought In Nearly $2 Billion," *The NonProfitTimes*, December 5, 2019.
[8] "US nonprofits raised $2.5 billion on #GivingTuesday in 2020," *Generocity*, December 21, 2020.

fitting The Reflect Organization, a national mental well-ness and suicide prevention nonprofit that has chapters at colleges and universities across the country. Thanks to the success of the original 3 Dollar Challenge, every dollar donated was matched (up to $75,000).

While $3 may seem insignificant, 3DC proved that every contribution—no matter how small—can make a difference.

Evidence that every penny helps can be found everywhere you look. People use crowdfunding platforms like GoFundMe, JustGiving, Fundly, and Facebook to receive personal donations for things such as medical bills, funerals, and education costs. Nonprofits use these platforms and other platforms like GoFundMe Charity, Classy, and PayPal to raise funds for all sorts of causes. What's great about crowdfunding is that it allows even the smallest contribution to work toward making a real, tangible difference.

When a friend's 22-year-old son, Darreck, was diagnosed with a rare brain cancer and died just months later, his family faced a crush of medical bills. To help, Darreck's girlfriend created a GoFundMe campaign to assist with the medical and funeral costs. The small donations that poured in from family and friends, many of whom were in their 20s themselves and had little to give, quickly added up to more than $16,000—enough to pay every bill and allow the family to focus on grieving their loss instead of worrying about the financial cost of the tragedy.

Often when I talk to someone about the power of giving, they tell a similar story. Whether you decide to give to individuals or put your gift to work to address a broader need, every penny really does help.

Too Many Choices

"I went down to the local coffee store
The menu went from the ceiling all the way
down to the floor
Decaf, cappuccino, or latte said the cashier
I said gimme a small cup of coffee and
let me get the hell up outta here"
— *Keb' Mo', 'Keep it Simple'*

We dream of having freedom of choice. But that freedom can quickly become a burden when the sheer number of choices makes decision-making near to impossible.

Starbucks advertises a menu of more than 80 *thousand* different drink combinations. Cheesecake Factory boasts a 21-page menu with more than 250 items (at last count). Netflix offers almost 6,000 titles (and some of us watched all of them during the pandemic!). Suddenly you're dizzy with options, and your brain simply can't pick.

We may want choices, but having fewer options actually makes it easier to choose.

I joke with my wealthier clients that one of their biggest challenges is 'choice anxiety'—the privileged struggle of having to decide whether to, say, play golf or spend the day on the boat. (If only we could all be faced with such tough decisions!) But every one of us can experience anxiety when we're forced to make a choice, and that can pose challenges for everything from dating to shopping to (you guessed it) giving.

Caltech looks at the perils of choice

In 2018, researchers at Caltech took a close look at how choice overload makes us feel—and behave. In the study,[9] volunteers were shown a menu of pictures to print on a coffee mug. The menu included 6, 12, or 24 pictures. They were asked to make a choice while researchers studied their brain activity using an MRI machine.

The MRI focused on activity in two specific regions of the brain: the anterior cingulate cortex, where the brain weighs cost and benefit, and the striatum, where the brain determines value. While it might seem intuitive that more choice would create more brain activity, that wasn't actually the case. Brain activity was actually highest when 12 choices were offered. Activity decreased when 6 choices were offered and (here's the surprise) when 24 were offered. Just like that massive menu at Cheesecake Factory, too many choices caused the brain to shut down. There was simply too much choice!

[9] "Choice overload reduces neural signatures of choice set value in dorsal striatum and anterior cingulate cortex," Reutskaja, E., Lindner, A., Nagel, R. *et al, Nature Human Behav*iour, 2018.

The National Center for Charitable Statistics reports that there are more than 1.5 million nonprofit organizations in the US alone. Just the menu of *types* of charities is big enough to make your head spin! Public and private charities. Private foundations. Religious organizations. Private schools. Chambers of commerce. Fraternal organizations. Civic leagues. Private fundraisers. Girl Scout Cookies!

So what's a giver to do?

Luckily, there are many (but not too many!) resources available to help you choose where to direct your giving. This list of four is a good place to start:

■ *Charity Navigator*
This online charity assessment tool (charitynavigator.com) doesn't narrow down the menu much—it includes information on more than 160,000 charities—but its Encompass Rating System does a great job of rating each organization based on factors such as finance and accountability, impact and results, leadership and adaptability, and culture and community. The easy-to-use menu offers some great 'Top 10' lists, including charities that have perfect scores, are 'super-sized' or celebrity-endorsed, rely on private contributions, or are 'worth watching.' If you're looking for a place to explore and learn, this is a great starting point.

■ *Chartered Advisor in Philanthropy® (CAP®)*
Advisors who hold a CAP designation have completed a program developed and administered by The American College of Financial Services. These specialists can offer valuable insights and tools to help you articulate and implement a philanthropic strategy based on your personal goals and objectives, analyze the effectiveness of specific charities and, ultimately, make choices that are right for you.

■ *Schwab Charitable®*

Schwab Charitable is a well-known charitable fund, but it also offers a great online tool (schwabcharitable.org/explore-charities) where you can search charities by specific cause, research, effectiveness, or background to help you choose where to give, however you choose to give.

■ *Community Foundations*

Community foundations are grantmaking public charities that focus on supporting people and causes in a specific geographic area. By helping community members pool their resources together, these foundations are able to create a greater local impact. Some, like the Jewish Community Foundation of Orange County (where I am proud to serve as a board member), also do a wonderful job at helping givers narrow their personal focus and choose which charities they want their dollars to support. To find a community foundation in your own community, visit the website for the Council on Foundations (cog.org/community-foundation-locator).

Many financial advisors (myself included) have a process of their own to help you narrow down the choices and align your giving with your own values. An advisor with experience in charitable giving can help you explore your values, identify the causes you care about most, and select the options that are right for you.

There are many—perhaps too many—choices when it comes to giving, but with a little homework and a little help, you can turn your freedom of choice into a powerful tool for change.

To learn more about tools to support your own charitable giving strategy, see Chapter 4.

Analysis Paralysis

"Just do it."
— *Nike*

The list of barriers to giving is endless—and it's different for everyone. The key to success is to recognize what's holding you back and make a change that leads to action.

In addition to the major barriers to giving that we've already talked about, overanalysis may be the most common barrier of all. If someone on the street asks you for money, do you hesitate because you wonder if your gift will be spent on the 'wrong' thing… on a beer rather than a meal? If an organization asks you for a donation, do you get hung up on the details of what percentage of your gift will be spent on the dreaded 'overhead' rather than directly to the cause?

You're not alone. If you ever have the opportunity to sit in on a board meeting for a charitable foundation, I promise you'll see analysis paralysis playing a role there, too. Perhaps giving, by its nature, asks us to question how our gifts will be used. I expect there's no way to turn off our human, analytic brains to help us convince ourselves we're giving 'right.'

But if all that thinking holds us back from giving, we need to take a new approach.

If over-analysis is preventing you from being a generous giver, it's time to proactively strip away the judgment and negative narratives you've learned in the past—to turn that thinking on its head—and strive to give without judgment and without the fear that you're giving 'wrong.' No giving can do harm. If you don't give, the alcoholic will find a way to drink. The addict will find a way to keep using. But how much good might your gift do? Often, you may not even know how much your gift is appreciated.

When gifts are hidden—even to the giver

Georgetown University Hospital in Washington D.C. has its own Hospital for Children that includes a pediatric cancer center. The moment you walk into the ward, you are struck by the quiet fear of the children—many who have been there for months—and their parents who are helpless except to give hugs and comfort to their kids in any way they can.

When my friend Carole was a college student, she volunteered as a storyteller there. One night a week, she would go sit with one child after another, reading to them in their hospital rooms to bring just a

little joy—to spend a half hour or so focused on something other than cancer.

One evening, after reading to a handful of the usual kids, she was heading out the door carrying an armful of picture books when a bedraggled looking dad stopped her and asked if she was the storyteller he'd heard about. He then went on to tell her how much her visits meant to his daughter—and to him. "She calls you her angel," he said, his eyes filling with tears. "But you're my angel too. When you come, it's the only time in the week when I can walk out of her room and know she'll be happy and smiling—if only for a little while."

When Carole shared her story with me, she told me that what surprised her most was how much her visits meant to this dad who was so grateful to be able to go grab a quick coffee without having to worry about his daughter. Just once a week. It was a gift she didn't even know she was giving.

No one wants a gift to be used poorly or squandered. But giving freely without worrying about the result may be the highest form of giving of all. That may come a little easier thanks to a recent study by Foundations for Social Change, a charitable organization based in Vancouver, in partnership with the University of British Columbia. As part of the group's *New Leaf Project*, researchers gave 50 homeless people $7,500 Canadian dollars (close to $6,000 US dollars), and then followed their lives over the next 12-18 months, comparing their outcomes to a control group that received no donations.

The results will make every dedicated giver smile.

About 70% of the people who received the cash gift were able to gain immediate access to food and find stable housing after one month—about a year faster than those who didn't receive the financial support. Plus, the recipients spent more on food, clothing, and rent, and there was a 39% decrease in spending on goods like alcohol, cigarettes, or drugs. Far from being squandered, the money was used for vital items. Rent. Food. Transportation (including buying a bike or paying for needed car repairs in order to get to work). Some recipients wanted to purchase computers or start their own small businesses. For the majority, the gift was a godsend that was used well and wisely.

While the Canadian study was small, the results are a strong reminder that it is often our own perceptions and fears—not reality—that can hold us back from giving. Barriers exist. We can find them anywhere we look. But in truth, the only insurmountable barrier is a lack of desire to give to others.

What's the antidote? Begin today to indoctrinate philanthropy into your daily life. Going back to Brian Armstrong's words: "Once a certain level of wealth is reached, there is little additional utility from spending more on yourself. One's ambition begins to move outwards." If you have enough resources to live comfortably, now is the time to share the wealth. If your resources are more limited, consider sharing your time and talent. If you can share time, talent, *and* treasure, even better! Decide who and how you want to help, create a plan, and start making it happen—today.

EXERCISE:

Narrow your focus areas

Exploring your focus areas can make it much easier to sidestep the barriers to giving.

The simplest way to organize your philanthropy is to focus on several specific causes that are personal and important to you, rather than giving across many issues. While your budget can certainly allow room for reactive and emergency giving, narrowing your focus areas for proactive giving can help prioritize your resources.

Activity E—Look back at your giving history helps you take stock of your past giving to identify any trends or themes. You can then determine which issues you are most passionate about, assess how you have supported these issues in the past, and decide whether you want to make adjustments in the future.

Activity F—Select your issues gives you the opportunity to begin with a clean slate, exploring a range of potential issues to support and then selecting those that align with your values and motivations.

Activity G—Craft your focus statements brings it all

together to help you identify what issues you want to address most, and the people and places you want to support through giving.

Activity H—Consider your time, talent & ties explores areas you may want to support by giving non-financial resources.

E
LOOK BACK AT YOUR GIVING & VOLUNTEERING HISTORY

Instructions

If you already have experience giving and volunteering, this exercise will help you identify trends and themes from your past to pinpoint your giving focus. From there, you can understand which issues you are most passionate about, assess how you have supported them, and decide whether you would like to make adjustments. If giving is new in your life—or you simply want to take a completely fresh approach—skip this exercise and move on to exercise F.

The following reflects my giving history from

_____ to

_____.

The following reflects my volunteering history from
_____ to
_____.

Instructions
Answer these questions based on your giving and
volunteering history:

Which organizations did you give to most frequently?

_____

_____

_____

_____

_____

Which organizations received most of your funding?

_____

_____

_____

_____

_____

To which organizations did you give the most time?

_____

_____

_____

_____

_____

_____

_____

_____

Which organizations do you want to continue to support with your charitable giving?

_____

_____

_____

_____

_____

_____

_____

Now that you have identified where you have been giving your money and time, consider if these are the causes you wish to support as you move forward with your philanthropy. Choose five causes that resonate the most with you at this time.

1:_____

2:_____

3:_____

4:_____

5:_____

For each of the causes you selected, you may wish to consider focusing on particular populations or geographies. For instance, if you aim to increase access to higher education, you may wish to choose a subset of a population, such as students from low socioeconomic backgrounds in a particular location. If you are unsure about the population or geography, you can add those details later.

F
BEGIN WITH A CLEAN SLATE

Instructions

The 'clean slate' approach enables you to identify broader causes or issues that concern you, regardless of your giving and volunteering history.

Select five causes from the list below you want to prioritize in your giving. If you want to give to causes not listed here, simply add your own.

ANIMAL PROTECTION & WELFARE

ARTS & CULTURE

CHILDREN & YOUTH SERVICES

CIVIL RIGHTS & ADVOCACY

CLIMATE CHANGE

CRIME PREVENTION

CRIMINAL JUSTICE REFORM

DISASTER PREPAREDNESS & RELIEF

EDUCATION

ENVIRONMENT

EQUALITY

FAMILY SERVICES & ASSISTANCE

FOOD & NUTRITION

HEALTH

HOUSING & HOMELESSNESS
HUMAN RIGHTS
INTERNATIONAL PEACE & SECURITY
LABOR UNIONS
LAW ENFORCEMENT
MEDICAL RESEARCH
MENTAL HEALTH
RACIAL JUSTICE
RECYCLING
POLLUTION
RELIGION
SOCIAL SERVICES
VOTER EDUCATION & REGISTRATION
WILDLIFE PRESERVATION & PROTECTION
WOMEN'S RIGHTS

1: _____

2: _____

3: _____

4: _____

5: _____

For each of the causes you selected, consider focusing
on particular populations or geographies. For instance,

if you aim to increase access to higher education, you may wish to choose a subset of a population, such as students from low socioeconomic backgrounds in a particular location. If you are unsure about the population or geography, you can add those details later.

G
CRAFT YOUR FOCUS STATEMENT

Instructions
A focus statement connects your values, motivations, and cause areas in a statement of philanthropic intent. A strong focus statement will help guide your charitable giving, especially in the face of competing demands. We recommend creating a separate focus statement for each cause you want to support.

Focus statement example
"I want to address education inequality for low-income secondary school students in the Los Angeles public schools because this aligns with my commitment to equity in public education."

Components of a focus statement
I want to address [What] for [Who] [Where] because this aligns with my commitment to [Which values].

What	What cause/issue do you want to address with your giving (e.g., environment, education, etc.)?
Who	Who will benefit from your giving (e.g., people experiencing homelessness, children from low-income backgrounds, abused animals)?
Where	Where, geographically, will you focus your giving (e.g., a specific location, locally, statewide, nationally, globally)?
Which values	Which values are driving your focus (e.g., respect, diversity, empathy)?

Create focus statements for the five causes you selected:

Focus statement 1:
I want to address _____
for _____
because this aligns with my commitment to
_____.

Focus statement 2:
I want to address _____
for _____
because this aligns with my commitment to
_____.

Focus statement 3:

I want to address _____

for _____

because this aligns with my commitment to

_____ .

Focus statement 4:

I want to address _____

for _____

because this aligns with my commitment to

_____ .

Focus statement 5:

I want to address _____

for _____

because this aligns with my commitment to

_____ .

H
CONSIDER YOUR TIME, TALENT & TIES

Financial 'treasure' is just one form of giving. You may also choose to give non-financial resources such as your time, talent, or ties. Volunteering can be an excellent way to learn more about your focus areas and get to know a particular organization. Many nonprofits post volunteer positions on their websites. It is common for organizations to announce a need for short-term commitments focused around a specific event or short-term business goal, as well as longer-term commitments connected to a series of events, an ongoing program, or extended strategic initiatives.

Another way to contribute at a leadership level is to serve on the board of a nonprofit organization. Board candidates are often selected based on the skills and expertise they can contribute. Board members may also be asked to serve as 'ambassadors' for the organization, tapping into their 'ties'—their social and professional networks—to help raise funds or other assistance. While board service can be very meaningful, it can also be a significant time commitment, depending on the needs of the organization and the skills and resources you and other board members bring to the table.

Instructions

Review the questions below to consider your interest in contributing your time, talent, and ties to a particular focus area. Write down your thoughts.

Is there an organization you would like to learn about through firsthand experience?

_____

_____

_____

_____

_____

_____

Is there a cause or organization that might benefit from your unique skills or experience?

_____

_____

_____

_____

_____

_____

_____

If you have a particular organization in mind, is that organization currently accepting volunteers? What responsibilities do volunteers have?

_____

_____

_____

_____

_____

_____

_____

How much time do you want to commit to an organization? Is that aligned with the organization's structure and requirements?

_____

_____

_____

_____

_____

_____

_____

Instructions

If you are interested in exploring serving on the board of an organization, consider these questions and write down your thoughts:

Do you have enough time for board service?
Serving as a board member requires more than attending meetings. You will often be expected to serve on one or more committees, read and understand financial documents, represent the organization at various events, and assist with fundraising.

_____

_____

_____

_____

_____

_____

_____

_____

_____

_____

Are you willing and able to meet fundraising expectations?
Board members are usually asked to make personal contributions as well as raise funds from their personal and professional networks. You may also be asked to network with potential donors on behalf of the organization.

_____

_____

_____

_____

What skills or expertise do you offer? Are your skills or expertise needed by the organization's board?
Board members offer a variety of skills and expertise to assist with the overall functions of the board and the organization. How you can make a difference in the organization depends on aligning what you offer with the organization's current needs.

_____

_____

_____

_____

_____

_____

How might you tap into your personal and professional networks to assist the organization in meeting its goals?

In addition to reaching out to friends and colleagues for fundraising parties or other special events, board members also often tap into their networks to seek advice and mobilize additional skill sets to assist with special projects and initiatives. Considering the organizations and causes in which you have a particular interest, who in your network comes to mind as a potential advocate? How might they be able to help support the goals of the organization?

_____

_____

_____

_____

_____

_____

_____

_____

_____

_____

_____

_____

CHAPTER 4

Strategies
for Giving

"Hope is not a strategy."
— *Vince Lombardi*

Giving is a simple act.

Without a plan, giving can help provide a meal, support a worthy cause, or provide comfort when it's needed in the moment.

You're moving forward, but you're steering blindly.

With a carefully designed strategy, giving can have much greater impact and create more meaningful change.

Your giving strategy is the key to charting a clear course forward and creating the change *you* want to see in the world.

Creating Impact

"Talent wins games, but teamwork
and intelligence win championships."
— *Michael Jordan*

Last November, I met with Linda to chat about her giving strategy for the year. While I've known her to be a generous giver over the years, I was thrilled to learn that she'd decided to increase her giving. And, as usual, she'd done her homework (and a lot of it!). When we sat down, she handed me a fat file folder with the details of the charities she wanted to support—all 17 of them.

Why the magic number of 17? (I was too curious not to ask!). She explained that when she'd decided to give $34,000 for the year, she loved the idea of dividing the money up, giving $2,000 to each charity equally.

Her giving was generous, and I definitely didn't want to dampen her enthusiasm. And yet I felt that she was missing out on an opportunity to do more… to create greater impact with fewer, larger gifts rather than many relatively smaller gifts. I took a deep breath, quietly slid her folder to the side—and began talking strategy.

No one would expect a sports team to win the season without strategy. And no one would invest in a company without a strategy (or at least I wouldn't recommend it). The reason: strategy works. While a lucky few achieve great heights by sheer chance, the more predictable path to success is to set short- and long-term goals, create a concrete plan to achieve those goals, and execute on that plan. It's that simple. That's true in sports. It's true in business. And it's true in the world of charitable giving.

When I shared my thoughts about the power of strategy with Linda and introduced the idea of contributing a larger amount to fewer organizations to create a greater, more targeted impact, she was very interested. As a highly successful entrepreneur, business strategy was in her blood. As a competitive tennis player, she was deeply familiar with the nuances of strategy on the court. She agreed it was time to grow her expertise in giving strategies.

She'd already done a good chunk of the work: in her folder were her detailed goals and values. These would dictate the kinds of organizations she wanted to support (the 17 she had chosen were a great starting point). She had a budget in place, too. She knew how much she wanted to give now, and she had included a projection for an annual increase based on the expected growth of her own income. The next step in building her strategy was to choose the best tools to help her achieve her goals.

And so we began. Our first step: to look at the menu.

As philanthropy has become more sophisticated, a variety of very smart tools have been created that can help boost the impact of philanthropic giving and make it easier than ever to give strategically. As a modern philanthropist, the options you choose will influence how you give, as well as your ability to increase your giving power. While the menu is constantly evolving, here's a quick look at the most common types, vehicles, and timeframes for giving (the *what*, *where*, and *when*), and ways to give smarter and more effectively (the *how*):

- *Types of Giving:*
  Cash | Real Estate | Appreciated Stock | Less Common Assets

- *Vehicles for Giving:*
  Donor-Advised Funds | Private Family Foundations
  Charitable Gift Annuities | Charitable Trusts

- *Timeframes for Giving:*
  Giving Now | Giving Now & Later | Giving Later

- *Smarter Giving:*
  Giving Circles | Corporate Matching Programs
  Community Foundations

It's a long list, I know. But a brief look at *what*, *where*, *when*, and *how* you can give (with a bit of *why* thrown into the mix) can help simplify the menu and help you make the right choices for you. Let's go...

Types of Giving

If you're like most people, your method of giving is probably quite simple. You either write a check to a chosen charity, donate food or unwanted clothes and household goods, or volunteer your time. But there are many other types of giving available. By expanding your knowledge of what you can give, you can stretch your giving power. An added bonus: you may be able to reduce your taxes to increase the resources you have to give.

Cash

Cold, hard cash. It's the most common form of giving. Whether you are writing a check each week to your synagogue or church, sending funds directly to a homeless shelter, or donating to become a member of your local public radio station, botanical garden, or other nonprofit, these donations are all considered cash gifts.

The benefit of gifting cash, of course, is that it's incredibly simple. You choose the recipient—either because you've been asked directly to contribute, or you choose the organization on your own—and you provide the funds. And there *can* be a tax benefit as well. If you itemize deductions on your taxes (which is much less common under the tax laws that came into effect with the 2017 Tax Cuts and Jobs Act) your tax deduction is equal to the amount of cash you donated, minus any services or merchandise you receive in return. The deduction is usually limited to 60 percent of your adjusted gross income (AGI).

In some cases, the direct benefits can be a lot of fun, too, including members-only galas and other events that attract donors with a bit of a wow factor. Plus, there is no confusing paperwork involved. All you need to do is give. But there is a downside. By simply giving cash, you are likely missing out on opportunities to stretch your giving power—either by reducing your taxable income (which, again, gives you more to give), or by empowering an organization with a gift that extends far beyond the current calendar year.

Don't get me wrong: gifting cash is important, and many organizations wouldn't survive without the cash donations they receive each year. In this way, cash really is king. But there are many ways to make your gift even more valuable. Read on!

Real Estate

Anyone who has ever inherited property is well aware of the tax implications that come with it. It may sound great that Uncle Kenny included you in his will, but unless you actually want to live at the property, selling it can be a major headache. And then there are the dreaded taxes. Many experts agree that estate tax rates are likely to increase in the near future, returning to more 'normal' levels of 55% or more. That's a lot of money going from Uncle Kenny straight to Uncle Sam.

As an enthusiastic philanthropist, you know there's a better solution: donating the property to charity.

When you donate property outright, the deed or title is transferred directly from your name to the charity, and you receive an immediate tax deduction equal to the fair market value of the property. If it isn't in your best interest to take the deduction immediately, you can carry it forward for up to five years. And, of course, you avoid paying the capital gains tax you would face if you sold the property.

Still living on a property that you want to give? No problem. You can arrange to have the deed transferred to the charity of your choice after your death—a move that will also lower your estate taxes because the value of the home will be removed from your estate. Uncle Kenny would be proud, your tax bill will thank you, and the recipient of your gift will be grateful for your generosity.

Appreciated Stock

Every investor is happy to see their stock portfolio grow. But there are times when that growth shifts from being a financial windfall to becoming a tax burden. That's when giving appreciated stock can help. Here are some options for tax-efficient gifting of stock:

■ *Donate appreciated securities directly to charity*

When you sell appreciated securities directly, you're bound to get hit with some hefty capital gains tax, which can significantly reduce the funds you have remaining to give. By donating your appreciated assets 'in kind' to a charity, the organization receives the actual stock (or other assets), rather than the proceeds from the sale of the assets. As a result, you save the federal capital gains tax, plus any state taxes. The donation also lowers your adjusted gross income (AGI), and if you itemize your taxes, you can include the market value of the donation as an itemized charitable contribution. This approach is good for the charity too. Because the stock was donated, as long as the organization is a qualified 501(c)(3) charity, any gains are tax-free. They can choose to hold on to the stock and allow them to continue to grow, or they can sell the stock without having to pay taxes on the gains. It's a win-win all around.

■ *Make a Qualified Charitable Distribution (QCD)*

If you are in a higher tax bracket, are 72 or older[10], and are taking Required Minimum Distributions (RMDs) from an IRA account, giving some or all of your annual distribution in the form of a Qualified Charitable Distribution (QCD) can save you a bundle in taxes while supporting your giving strategy. If you give the full amount to charity, you will pay ZERO taxes on your RMD. And because taxes were deferred on the money that went into the account, every penny is 100% tax free. Here's how it works in the real world:

Eric is 72 years old and has an IRA at Charles Schwab with a $20,000 RMD. Using a QCD, he makes a donation to two different charities: $5,000 to his church and $5,000 to the Children's Hospital of Orange County. Schwab writes three checks: two checks for $5,000 are sent directly to Eric's selected charities for them to use tax-free, and he receives a third check for the remaining $10,000 of his RMD. Because only the amount he receives personally is taxable, Eric is able to cut his RMD taxes in half, and the charities he cares about receive a substantial sum—tax free.

The annual limit for QCDs is very high—$100,000—and every dollar you give is excluded from your adjusted gross income. If you want to increase your giving power, there's an added perk: you can use a QCD to give up to the $100,000 limit every year, <u>even if that amount exceeds your annual RMD.</u>

---

[10] Per the SECURE Act of 2020, RMDs must be withdrawn annually starting with the year you reach 72 (70 ½ if you reached 70 ½ before January 1, 2020), or, if later, the year in which you retire. However, if the retirement plan account is an IRA or you are a 5% owner of the business sponsoring the retirement plan, the RMDs must begin once you reached age 72 (70 ½ if you reach 70 ½ before January 1, 2020), regardless of whether you are retired.

■ *Name a charity as your IRA beneficiary*

If outliving your retirement savings is a real fear, you may want to consider donating the remainder of your IRA to a named charity at your death. Though you receive no tax benefits using this approach, your heirs will: the IRA amount will not be subject to estate tax, and they will not have to pay any income tax on the donated funds. You can also rest easy knowing that you are giving only what you don't need during your own lifetime.

Having a bundle of appreciated stock is a good problem to have, but it can be a real problem in some cases—especially when you are flooded with a large amount of highly appreciated securities and face an unwanted tax hit. Because nonprofits are not required to pay taxes on these assets, they are more than happy to take them off your hands. In this case, appreciated stock can be a truly perfect gift.

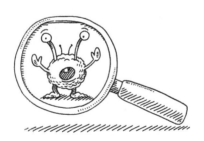

Less Common Assets

There are other assets that can boost your giving power that you may not even realize you can give. These non-cash assets are often overlooked, but they, too, can help fuel a needy cause.

The most obvious method of giving non-cash assets is to donate unneeded clothes and household goods to well known thrift-store-based charities like Goodwill, Salvation Army, Veterans Affairs, or Oxfam. As a result, these organizations sometimes get more than they bargained for when donors give what may be their oddest 'treasures.' At the top of the list of the strange (and somehow wonderful!) donations received in recent years are a prosthetic leg, a sheep's head, and a live ferret. But even the bizarre can sometimes be valuable—such as the antique purse carved in the shape of a samurai that was donated to the British Heart Foundation. A true treasure, the item was auctioned off, raising more than $1,500 for the charity. But even if you don't have a goldmine of antiques hiding in the back of your closet, you may want to consider these other types of non-cash assets to support your giving strategy:

■ *Fine Art & Collectibles*

Depending on how you obtained a particular piece of fine art or a valuable collectible, selling it could result in a higher capital gains tax rate (as much as 28%) compared to other types of assets. To reduce or eliminate capital gains taxes and increase the value of your gift, individual pieces or entire collections can be donated directly to your own Donor-Advised Fund or other qualified charity. (Read more about Donor-Advised Funds in the next section.) But taxes aren't the only thing you need to think about. Selling collectibles, either before or after giving them, can be tricky. I have a friend who has been collecting first-edition Marvel comic books for decades. Even though the value has jumped thanks to the popularity of the Marvel movie franchise, finding buyers willing to pay even close to the full 'value' took over a year. Don't assume the actual value until the sale is complete!

Donating appreciated art to a Donor-Advised Fund

Martin and Eva were planning to sell a painting they inherited from Eva's family and then contribute the proceeds to their Donor-Advised Fund. The painting was valued at $1 million, with a cost basis of $75,000. But the sale would have resulted in long-term capital gains taxes of nearly $300,000.

Instead, I recommended they donate the piece directly to the fund <u>before</u> selling it, and then put the piece up for auction after it was an asset of the fund. The approach added additional funds to their Donor-Advised Fund and saved them thousands of dollars in taxes.

■ Privately Held Business Interests

If retirement is on the horizon, consider gifting a portion of your interest in a privately held company (a C-Corp, S-Corp, LP, or LLC). Donating your business interest <u>before</u> the sale can reduce your tax burden and boost the value of your gift.

■ Cryptocurrency

Remember Brian Armstrong's charity Coinbase from Chapter 2? It's not the only organization that accepts bitcoin donations. You can give cryptocurrency to a Donor-Advised Fund or other public charity that will accept it (not all do). Just keep in mind that the IRS doesn't qualify this type of asset as legal-tender currency.[11] From a tax perspective, that means gifts of cryptocurrency are treated as either capital assets or income (depending on whether the cryptocurrency was held for investment purposes or received as a form of compensation).

■ *Cars and Boats*

It is surprisingly easy to give cars and boats to charity. My local NPR station advertises that it will pick up any vehicle—whether it works or not—and take care of all the paperwork, including transferring the title and appraising the value for tax purposes. They are just one of many nonprofits that make donating a car or boat extremely easy. To give, consider ItsDonated, Vehicles For Veterans, and Boat Angel.

■ *Miles and Points*

If you are a frequent flyer with more airline miles or hotel points than you can possibly use, most loyalty programs offer the option to give your miles and points directly to charity. The Make-A-Wish° Foundation and a handful of other nonprofits specialize in collecting donated frequent flyer miles, and almost every airline and hotel chain allows members to donate to selected charities directly from their own websites. The only downfall: because the IRS sees donated points and miles as gifts from the airline or hotel, there is no tax deduction for you. But you're still doing good!

---

[11] Under Notice 2014-21 and the October 2019 Frequently Asked Questions published by the IRS, cryptocurrency is generally considered "virtual currency" and treated as property. Tax principles related to property transactions apply to transactions involving cryptocurrency. To the extent that bitcoin is held for investment purposes, it is generally treated as a capital asset, and any resulting gains and losses are characterized as capital.

Vehicles for Giving

Once you know *what* you want to give, you need to decide *where* to give. There are a variety of vehicles for giving, each with its own advantages. Depending on how much you have to give, when you prefer to see the tax benefits of giving, your unique giving priorities, and other factors, one or more of the following options can help bring your strategy to life.

Donor-Advised Funds

One of the most popular giving tools today is the Donor-Advised Fund. Managed by a third-party sponsor (a nonprofit organization, for-profit financial firm, or community foundation), this type of fund offers some great tax benefits, as well as a high level of flexibility and low costs.

How popular are they? Grants from Donor-Advised Funds to quali-fied charities totaled more than $25 billion in 2019—a 93% increase since 2015.[12] And there are good reasons for their popularity. Not only are Donor-Advised Funds, or DAFs, considerably cheaper than Private Family Foundations (see the next section to learn more), but they offer other very important benefits to givers.

I've heard these funds referred to as a sort of marriage between a private foundation and a mutual fund. It makes sense. Once your assets—which can include cash, company shares, and even real estate—are in a DAF, the fund is professionally managed by the sponsoring institution, but at a fraction of the cost you would pay as a Private Family Foun-dation. That means your money is invested and managed by experts (similar to a mutual fund), but you maintain a high degree of control over how your funds are distributed. Because a DAF is held within the sponsor organization, you get to recommend how your funds are invested and granted, but the sponsor organization is ultimately re-sponsible for final approval of donor requests.

Donating appreciated stock vs. using a DAF

I can hear your question already: why use a DAF instead of simply donating inherited or appreciated stock? The answer lies in how much flexibility you want within your giving strategy.

Liz is a great example. When her tech startup was acquired last summer, part of the agreement was a massive block of highly appreciated stock. Since it had to be cashed out, she would have been hit with a huge tax

---

[12] "The 2020 DAF Report," National Philanthropic Trust.

bill. If she donated the stock, she would have had to do-nate the full amount in one fell swoop. Instead, she estab-lished a DAF. Because she is still figuring out the details of her giving strategy, creating a DAF bought her time since she can distribute the funds whenever she chooses. And once she has decided where she wants to give and when, she can set the schedule according to her own wishes rather than letting the IRS dictate her approach. She can even set up the funds to continue even after her death.

For dedicated givers (which I hope, by now, includes you!), the Donor-Advised Fund may be the new king.

The tax benefits of Donor-Advised Funds are great, too. Contributions to a DAF are tax deductible in the year they are made, and the limit is HUGE. You can donate up to 60% of your adjusted gross income (AGI) every year. This makes it a particularly useful tool if you've received a large inheritance, a lump of appreciated stock, or any other financial windfall that could deliver a painful tax hit. Also, there is no annual payout requirement from the IRS, giving you complete freedom to decide when you want to give. And because DAFs do not require tax returns, administrative costs are lower, and it is much easier to give anonymously—an important benefit if you prefer to protect your privacy when it comes to which charities you support.

Donor-Advised Funds are also transferrable to your heirs, and inherited funds can even be gifts to other DAFs. After Laura's mother died, Laura acquired control over her mom's DAF, but she hadn't changed the name on the fund to her own. She was continuing to give generously through the DAF, but every gift she gave named her mother as the donor. It was confusing to everyone involved. Laura was thrilled when I told her that, as the heir of the DAF, she could simply gift the remainder of the funds to the DAF she and her husband already had in place. Suddenly, giving became so much easier!

Perhaps the biggest benefit of a Donor-Advised Fund is that it supports a more proactive approach to giving. Rather than giving reactively by writing a check that comes out of your current income, a Donor-Advised Fund offers a higher level of sophistication to support a giving strategy that lasts a lifetime—and can even extend to future generations.

Private Family Foundations

If your giving budget is particularly high and one of your top priorities is ensuring your giving strategy is completely aligned with your family's values, a Private Family Foundation may be right for you.

For families with substantial wealth, a Private Family Foundation provides total control over where funds are directed. That's quite different from Donor-Advised Funds that are *advised* by, but not *owned* or *controlled* by, the donors. I like to think of Private Family Foundations as a personal piggy bank for families that are deeply involved in the giving process and are committed to supporting causes that matter to them personally.

Typically created as perpetual endowments that are designed to last for generations, Private Family Foundations support a much wider variety of giving than nearly any other vehicle. Think individual and international grants, scholarships and fellowships, and other direct charitable activities. They also are able to hold all sorts of assets. In addition to tangible assets like cash and securities, Private Family Foundations can hold real estate, as well as intangible personal property, such as patents, copyrights, and partnership interests. In contrast to Donor-Advised Funds, Private Family Foundations are set up as charitable trusts or corporations and retain full control of donated assets. Another important upside of a Private Family Foundation is that it offers a larger tax deduction based on AGI (adjusted gross income).

But there are some downsides, too. First, Private Family Foundations can be relatively expensive to administer. They have the ability to support employees (which points to the fact that you may need employees to make them effective!), which is why they often exist hand-in-hand with family offices (privately held wealth management firms that are owned and operated by a single family). The regulations and tax laws are also stricter, there are mandatory annual distributions, and all donations made by the foundation are publicly reported—which means your charitable activities cannot be kept under wraps, even when you want them to be.

Private Family Foundations vs. Donor-Advised Funds

So why does a Private Family Foundation make sense for some families, while a Donor-Advised Fund makes the most sense for others?

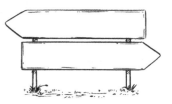

The three biggest deciding factors are control, taxes, and costs. A Private Family Foundation allows the highest level of control over your assets—like a private piggy bank. A Donor-Advised Fund offers less control, but it provides immediate tax benefits. And, of course, a Private Foundation is more expensive to operate. Your financial advisor can help you look at the specific details to understand which option is most aligned with your overall giving strategy.

One of the key advantages of a Private Family Foundation is that it can fill the gap to address a charitable mission that is not being tackled by an existing nonprofit. A great example of this is the Livestrong Foundation. Lance Armstrong's public battle with testicular cancer put a face to the disease. The American Cancer Society had been around since 1913, but Armstrong felt the organization wasn't doing enough to eradicate cancer. He created the Lance Armstrong Foundation in 1997 with the specific goal of improving the lives of cancer survivors and those affected by cancer. The nonprofit was rebranded as Livestrong in 2003 and continues to be a major contributor to cancer-related research, generating more than $500 million worth of funds.[13] In 2020, the foundation vowed to spend $5-6 million annually to

---

[13] Science News Daily, January 2013.

support entrepreneurs developing products to improve treatment and patient care.

Other well-known examples are the Bill and Melinda Gates Foundation, whose mission is to "help all people lead healthy, productive lives"; the Nobel Foundation, whose sole mission is to ensure a secure financial standing for the Nobel Prize over the long term, and that the institutions that award the prize are "guaranteed independence in their work of selecting participants"; and the Samueli Foundation, which invests in "innovative, entrepreneurial, and sustainable ideas." These organizations each work to fulfill a unique mission that is not addressed by any other nonprofit in the world.

Not every Private Family Foundation has such a targeted mission, and not every one of the 44,000+ Private Foundations in the US boasts an exceptional level of wealth. In 2019, 67% of all Private Foundations in the US had less than $1 million.[14] If you have the means to support a Private Family Foundation and your family has a specific charitable mission you want to support over generations, a Private Family Foundation may be just the ticket.

---

[14] "Revealing The 'Invisible' 98% of Private Foundations," Forbes, June 2019.

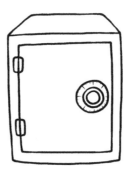

Charitable Gift Annuities

Even if you're absolutely gung-ho about a particular charity and want to support it in every way you can, you don't want to put your own livelihood at risk. (I would never, ever recommend that you give more than you can afford or risk your retirement, no matter how worthy the cause!) If you're concerned about protecting your own financial health during your lifetime, a Charitable Gift Annuity can help.

This unique type of gift involves a contract between you and a particular charity that requires you to transfer cash or property to the nonprofit. In return, you receive a partial tax deduction plus a guaranteed stream of income for the rest of your life. When you die, whatever remains of your gift goes directly to the charity. It is the 'gift that keeps on giving.'

A gift to Hadassah delivers income for life

A Charitable Gift Annuity worked perfectly for Terry. She wanted to support a charity that meant a lot to her: Israel's Hadassah University Hospital. But because she was in perfect health, she worried that giving too much could put her at risk of outliving her savings. Using a Charitable Gift

Annuity, Terry entered into a contract with
Hadassah. In return for her large cash gift
to the hospital, she receives 8% in income
from the annuity each year for the rest of
her life—more than enough to maintain her
lifestyle. When she dies, which could be
in 5 years or 20, Hadassah will receive the
remainder of the annuity as a charitable donation.

The annuity made sense from a tax perspective as well.
Terry received a partial tax deduction for her donation.

Depending on the charity, a charitable gift annuity can be funded with cash donations, and often with securities and gifts of personal property as well. And though the minimum amount for establishing a charitable gift annuity may be as low as $5,000, in my experience, that's pretty rare. Most charities require a much larger initial donation. In general, charitable gift annuities make the most sense for higher-net worth individuals and couples who choose to give a significant portion of their assets to a single charity but want the security of annual income for life.

Charitable Gift Annuities can also be valuable estate-planning tools. If you have considerable wealth, making a large donation through a Charitable Gift Annuity can reduce the size of your estate and, ultimately, reduce estate taxes for your heirs. You can also donate appreciated stock which, as you already know, can eliminate capital gains taxes that would otherwise be paid by you or your heirs.

If you have more liquid assets than you need in your lifetime, have a single charity you want to support, and want to ensure guaranteed income for life, explore whether your chosen charity offers the option of a Charitable Gift Annuity.

Charitable Trusts

There are two types of charitable trusts that may be interesting components of your financial plan—a charitable lead trust (CLT) and a charitable remainder trust (CRT).

■ *A charitable lead trust (CLT)* is established by transferring assets into a trust and donating a stream of income from those assets to a charitable organization each year. The trust can be structured so that you either receive annual income, or you receive an estate tax deduction on the donated assets. After the income stream period ends (this can be set to be either at the time of death or after a predetermined number of years) the remaining assets are distributed to beneficiaries of the trust.

What is unique about a CLT is that it performs well in a low-interest-rate environment. In short, the lower the federal interest rate, the higher the income (to the donor as well as the charity). If you choose to receive a gift tax deduction rather than income, a low interest rate will deliver a higher tax deduction. The money that remains at the end of the terms of the trust can be distributed to other beneficiaries or held in the trust, and you receive an immediate gift tax deduction based on the value of the income stream to the charity. A CLT can be a great tool for transferring wealth to your heirs, while also providing consistent cash flow to the charity of your choice. The only real disadvantage is that it requires annual administrative management, which can be costly.

■ *A charitable remainder trust (CRT)* is similar to a charitable lead trust, but with one big difference: in a CRT, the beneficiaries and donor are paid *first*, receiving their stream of income before the charitable organization does. This can be a great way to convert appreciated assets into income, while continuing to support your giving strategy.

With a CRT, you receive an income stream from the trust for a term of years or for the rest of your life, and the charity receives the remaining trust assets at the end of that term. You also receive an immediate income tax deduction when the CRT is funded, based on the current value of the contributed assets. This is a great option if you have highly appreciated investments but want to maintain a predictable flow of personal income, while also providing a consistent flow of cash to charity. Like a CLT, the main disadvantage is the cost of the annual administration of the trust.

Many of my clients have found that combining a Donor-Advised Fund with a charitable lead trust or charitable remainder trust supports their long-term giving strategy. Naming the Donor-Advised Fund as the lead beneficiary on either type of trust allows you to maintain control over how charitable funds are distributed—both during your lifetime and after your death. If these options interest you, speak with a financial advisor experienced in charitable giving strategies to get the ball rolling.

Timeframes for Giving

Another important aspect of any giving strategy is choosing *when* to give. Whether you give now, later, or now *and* later will influence which giving vehicles are most appropriate to support your strategy. Depending on the size of your giving budget and your other financial resources, the timing of your giving may also have an important impact on your personal income and your ability to support and sustain your lifestyle throughout your lifetime. And if leaving a lasting legacy is a goal, giving at the right time using the right vehicle can help strengthen and support your legacy for generations.

Giving Now

Urgent need is one of the main reasons to give *now*. Without the help of annual giving, many organizations would not have the resources to fulfill their missions. At worst, many nonprofits would disappear completely without the ongoing support of givers like you. If you choose to give now, look to cash, appreciated stock, and charitable trusts to support your giving strategy.

As I touched on in Chapter 1, giving a percentage of your earnings is an aspect of the religious practice of Devout Philanthropy. *Tzedakah*, a fundamental concept in the Jewish faith, is a moral obligation to give at least 10% of your earnings to help the needy. The Christian faith also follows the custom of giving 10% of your income each year as part of *tithing*. The Muslim tradition of *Zakat* is slightly different, requiring Muslims with assets that exceed a certain level (the *nisab*) to give 2.5%, or 1/40, of their total wealth, including income, savings, and all other property and investments. Judaism, Christianity, and Islam all ask their followers to give within the calendar or lunar year. In other words, they are required to give *now*.

Whether you are following the guidance of your faith or simply have the desire to support charitable causes every year, there are many vehicles on the menu that make sense.

■ *Cash*

Cash is appreciated by any charity at any time. Not only is cash often the easiest resource to give, but depending on your tax situation and the current tax laws, giving cash may offer some level of tax benefit to help reduce your current-year tax bill.

■ *Appreciated Stock*

One of the primary reasons many givers choose to give appreciated stock in the first place is to eliminate capital gains tax. Because qualified nonprofits are not required to pay this sometimes hefty tax, donating your appreciated stock now can provide much-needed support when and where it's needed.

■ **Charitable Trusts**

Both charitable lead trusts (CLTs) and charitable remainder trusts (CRTs) give you the freedom to give generously now while providing a level of guaranteed income. If you want to give generously now but are concerned about maintaining a steady source of income for the rest of your life, a charitable trust may be an ideal option.

Giving Now & Later

Some of the most effective giving strategies rely on a combination of tools and timeframes to offer different types of charitable support while creating a high level of tax efficiency. Donor-Advised Funds, Private Foundations, and Charitable Gift Annuities all provide flexible giving strategies that allow you to give when you choose—both now and later.

■ **Donor-Advised Funds**

From a timing perspective (and many other perspectives), Donor-Advised Funds are probably the most flexible tool out there. Once you establish your DAF, you have the freedom to both *contribute* additional assets now and later, and to *give* now or later. The choice is yours. And whatever is left in your DAF at the time of your death can be transferred to your heirs.

■ *Private Foundations*

Private Foundations offer many of the same benefits, making it easy to give now and later. However, the IRS does require Private Foundations to distribute 5% of the 'fair market value of their assets each year.' Some foundations give only what's required, others (the majority) give far more than the minimum, while some make it their mission to drain their funds entirely every year.

■ *Charitable Gift Annuities*

Because Charitable Gift Annuities are based on an immediate transfer of assets to a charity but also provide a guaranteed income stream for the rest of your life, they can be a great way to give now and later—with no risk to your own lifestyle or wellbeing.

Giving Later

There are a few reasons some givers choose to wait to give until the end of life. Remember Isadore Myers in Chapter 3? As a skilled money manager, Izzy chose to invest and grow his wealth while he was living in order to create the greatest charitable impact after his death.

A more common reason to give later is the very real fear of outliving your savings. Having recently lived through one of the greatest economic crises in a century, you may want to be 100% certain you have enough resources to sustain you and your family in the face of any future crisis (including something as dramatic as a global pandemic!).

Whatever your reasons may be, giving later is a very safe and generous way to give. And because your gift is likely to have grown over time, your gift may be greater than anything you could have afforded to give during your lifetime. If you choose to give later, Charitable Reverse Mortgages and Legacy Gifts are great tools to have in your toolkit.

■ *Charitable Reverse Mortgages*

While you can certainly donate real estate before your death (a particularly smart move if you have inherited property and want to avoid capital gains taxes), a Charitable Reverse Mortgage is a lesser-known option that can provide a stable income source and enable you to give to the charity of your choice later. This approach basically combines a Charitable Gift Annuity with what's called a Retained Life Estate that allows you to transfer the title of your home and continue to live there (or rent the property out) for the rest of your life. At the time of your death, the property is passed on to the charity of your choice. The charity can then sell the property and bank the proceeds—all without paying any capital gains or other taxes on the real estate. In the interim, you or your designee receives an annual fixed income. In addition to the yearly payout, you receive a tax deduction for the difference between the remainder value of your home and the value of the payout. This can be a great option if you want to donate real estate later and ensure a level of guaranteed income today.

■ *Legacy Gifts*

'Creating a legacy' is something lots of people talk about. Who doesn't want to leave behind some sort of lasting impact on the world? But making it happen in a concrete, tangible way can be a challenge. That's where Legacy Gifts come in.

A Legacy Gift is a donation you make after your death. Usually designed to reflect your values, it is often considered the last—and most lasting—act of charitable giving. Legacy Gifts are commonly used to build endowments to provide an ongoing source of income for an organization each year in perpetuity. That means that long after you are gone, your gift will continue to support the values that mattered most to you during your life. Legacy Gifts are quite simple, too, because they don't require tons of paperwork or financial details. You can leave a Legacy Gift in the most basic Will, through a Trust, or by naming an organization as your beneficiary designation on your IRA, 401(k), or other financial account. Most Legacy Gifts are based on one thing: a simple promise.

Remember The Giving Pledge that was created by Bill Gates, Melinda French Gates, and Warren Buffet? (If you skipped ahead, read more about it in Chapter 3.) This sort of promise to give posthumously is not reserved for the ultra-rich. The promise to give a Legacy Gift can be made by anyone—no matter how much or how little you have to give.

At the Jewish Community Foundation of Orange County, we introduced a Legacy Gifts program over a decade ago. We asked individuals and families to sign the 'Endowment Book of Life' where they state their intent to provide a Legacy Gift, as well as honor their family and values with a personal statement written in the book. Similar to the Giving Pledge, it helps givers clarify their own values and then leave a gift that helps ensure those values are honored long after their own death. So far, thousands of people throughout North America have made the promise to make a Legacy Gift in the Endowment Book of Life.

This is just one example of how a Legacy Gift can be used to continue supporting your values after you're gone. This type of promise begins with a conversation about what you want to see survive in the future and how your gift can help make that wish a reality. Involving your children and grandchildren in the conversation about your promise can strengthen your legacy even more by influencing funding by future generations. You can create a Legacy Gift for any cause that supports your values, wishes, and dreams for the future.

Smarter Giving

Everyone wants to be smarter, right? In the world of giving, one of the smartest things you can do is create a real, long-term strategy that is built to fit your philanthropic goals, your resources, and your personal preferences. But even with a great strategy that puts the right tools to work to support your goals, there are three more things that can help you boost your impact and take your giving to a whole new level: Giving Circles, Community Foundations, and Corporate Matching Programs.

Giving Circles

Giving Circles are one of my favorite ways to give wisely.

For years, my wife Jeanne and I were part of a Giving Circle. A couple of times each year, we would meet with a handful of other families who had all agreed to donate a certain amount to a general pool of funds. We would share ideas and perspectives, and then decide together which charities we wanted to support with a donation. It was a powerful way to give. All of our kids were included in the conversations and participated in the decision-making process, so it was a great exercise for them (and for the adults, too). Why should we give to one charity instead of another? What makes a certain cause more—or less—important to each person in the circle? These are questions that every modern philanthropist needs to explore. By asking them together, we were able to hear different perspectives and make decisions together based on feedback from everyone in the circle. And, of course, by combining our funds, we were able to create a greater impact on each charity we chose to support. It was a powerful inspiration for everyone involved.

Creating a Giving Circle can be as easy as bringing together like-minded givers who are interested in pooling funds and working as a collective. You can also join an established Giving Circle in your community. In my area, the Orange County United Way offers four different Giving

Circles to fit the style and interests of each giver. You can find Giving Circles in most major cities and many smaller communities.

There are now more than 1,600 in the US today, and that number is growing every day.[15] Whatever your own passion may be, there is likely a Giving Circle dedicated to serving the cause. In Chapter 2, I mentioned that my daughter Beaue was part of a Giving Circle called the Young Philanthropists Group that is just for teens. There is the NEID Giving Circle that focuses on racial injustice and climate change. New York has an Asian Women Giving Circle, and Amplifier is a network of Giving Circles based on Jewish values. In Washington, D.C., Black Benefactors focuses its giving on Black-led nonprofits, the Liberated Capital provides rapid response to Native Americans in need of emergency support, and the LGBTQ Latinx Giving Circle supports inclusion and acceptance for members of the LGBTQ community.

If you can't find a Giving Circle that matches your interests, simply create a Giving Circle to fill the gap. To learn how to create one, check out the great resources at amplifiergiving.org.

---

[15] "Giving Circles: A Growing Force for Democratizing Philanthropy," Nonprofit Quarterly, December 2020.

Community Foundations

As you can probably guess by the name, a Community Foundation is a public charity designed to focus on the needs of a specific community. Unlike a Private Family Foundation which is established, funded, and governed by a single family or other small group, a Community Foundation relies on donations from the public, and is managed and governed by a diverse board of directors.

If you want the giving power of a Private Family Foundation but not the hassle of managing a fund on your own, a Community Foundation is an alternative that offers many of the advantages of a Private Foundation—with none of the headaches.

The humble beginnings of the Community Foundation

The first Community Foundation was established in 1914 by Frederic Goff, a highly respected banker at the Cleveland Trust Company. His vision: "to pool the charitable resources of Cleveland's philanthropists, living and dead, into a single, great, and permanent endowment for the betterment of the city. Community leaders would then forever distribute the interest that the trust's resources would accrue to fund such charitable purposes as will best make for the mental, moral, and physical improvement of the inhabitants of Cleveland."

It was an ambitious goal, to be sure. Even so, I have no doubt that the results far exceeded Goff's initial expectations. In 2020, The Cleveland Foundation awarded more than 5,500 grants worth more than $131 million and received more than $100 million in new gifts.  And the reach of the vision didn't stop there. More than a hundred years later, there are now more than 800 community foundations operating across the US, each actively addressing needs of their own community.

With a focus on the needs of local people and causes, Community Foundations often support nonprofits that impact the immediate community: homeless shelters, hospitals, the arts, and more. This makes them living examples of the mantra "think globally, act locally." But they are by no means restricted to local charities. As an individual donor, you can choose where to direct your giving—even if the organizations you choose to support exist far beyond your local community.

And though Community Foundations are funded by a group of local individuals, families, and businesses, they are structured to support a uniquely individual style of giving, allowing you to define your own philanthropic mission statement, create your own giving plan, and direct your funds toward causes and nonprofits that matter most to you. In fact, one of the biggest benefits of giving through a Community Foundation is that these organizations can help you define your plan and put it into action. If you want guidance, they offer one-to-one assistance from experienced teams of philanthropists and professionals whose insights can be an especially valuable resource.

Community Foundations are an important part of the communities they serve. That can be an added benefit as a modern philanthropist. Your Community Foundation can be a great place to meet other like-minded people who have made giving a priority in their own lives. Donor events range from basic informational sessions to extravagant galas hosted by generous donors. You can choose to be a very active participant or a rather quiet contributor—whatever style suits you best.

In my area, two prominent Community Foundations are the Orange County Community Foundation and the Jewish Community Foundation of Orange County where I have served on the board of directors for a number of years. To find a Community Foundation in your own neck of the woods, the Council on Foundations offers an easy-to-use Community Foundation locator on their website at cof.org.

Corporate Matching Programs

What if you could double every dollar you give? It's every giver's dream come true. And if you're lucky enough to work for a company that offers a corporate matching program, you can make that dream a reality today.

My friend Jay works at Google, and I was thrilled when he called me last year and told me he wanted to take advantage of Google Matching Gifts, the company's generous corporate matching program. The program matches employee donations up to $10,000 per donor per year, and for every hour an employee volunteers, Google provides a $10 grant to the nonprofit. Google even supports fundraising event contributions; if an employee participates in an existing event (think AIDS/Lifecycle, Komen-Race for a Cure, the Pan-Mass Challenge) or organizes one of their own, Google will match up to $12,000 each year. What an opportunity!

Of course, I was even happier when Jay told me he wanted to give to a cause that was important to *me*. So the first time he used the match, he contributed to our Blaze Bernstein Memorial Fund (an example of a fund created with the help of a Community Foundation)—and doubled his gift.

But he didn't stop there. I have no idea if Jay came from a family of givers, but once he got a taste of what it was like to give, he became an enthusiastic modern philanthropist. Since that first donation, he has continued to take full advantage of Google Matching Gifts to support a variety of causes. And he no longer needs me to point him toward something that matters. I've watched him blossom into a connoisseur of charitable giving, even hosting a table at Google's charitable giving fair featuring my son's memorial fund. (As Jay told me, he's ready to #BlazeItForward!) Jay's newfound enthusiasm as a giver is, at least in part, thanks to Google's mission of philanthropy.

Does your employer offer a matching gift program? If you're not sure, you're not alone. According to Double the Donation, a promoter of corporate matching programs, while 65% of Fortune 500 companies offer matching gift programs, 78% of match-eligible donors have no idea that their company offers a matching gift program. Double the Donation estimates that $4-$10 billion in matching gift funds go un-claimed every year, and only 7% of donors at companies that do offer matching gift programs actually take the time to submit a matching gift request and take advantage of FREE MONEY!

No matter what you do in life, if you work for a corporation, ask if a corporate matching program is available. If it is, don't be one of the 93% of employees who don't request a match. Make a donation, get the match, and double your donation to your favorite nonprofit.

Picking the Right Tool

Do you own a multitool? Whether or not you carry one in your pocket at all times (preparation is everything!) or have one stashed away in a drawer ready to come to the rescue at a moment's notice, these miniature toolboxes are great for anyone who wants to have the right tool at the right time.

While it may not be as compact and cool looking as a Leatherman or a good-old Swiss Army knife, you can think of the collection of tools and techniques in this chapter as your 'giving multitool,' putting the right tool at your fingertips when you need to get a job done. The next step is to decide which options are right for you to accomplish your personal goals. It's time to refine your strategy and choose *what*, *where*, *when*, and *how* to bring it to life.

Making those choices is rarely as easy as choosing between that tiny little pocket knife or the miniature saw blade. I've already shared many of the reasons why you might choose some options over others, but here are some other basics that can help you narrow down the menu to choose the most appropriate tool for the job:

■ *Are you concerned about cost, tax liability, or grant-making limitations?*

While many of the tools address these issues at some level, a Donor-Advised Fund can be particularly effective at reducing costs and complexity and maximizing immediate tax benefits, while protecting your privacy by supporting anonymous giving. A Private Foundation is more expensive and complex and stretches tax benefits over time. And though your contributions are made public through the foundation's tax returns, they offer greater flexibility in how you put your charitable funds to work, and they are more useful for engaging future generations to continue your legacy. If *all* of these factors are important, you can use *both* tools at the same time to support your giving strategy.

■ *Do you need guaranteed income?*

If you want to give during your lifetime but want to ensure some level of guaranteed income, Charitable Trusts and Charitable Gift Annuities can be great options. You can create either of these through an irrevocable transfer of cash or other property, and both tools can be combined with a Donor-Advised Fund to boost your giving flexibility and help establish a legacy.

■ *Do you want to reduce your gift or estate taxes?*

If your goal is to give during your lifetime and stretch your resources by reducing gift and estate taxes, consider creating a Donor-Advised Fund and then naming it as the lead beneficiary for a Charitable Lead Trust.

■ *Is guidance and becoming part of a community of givers important?*

Whether you are new to giving or simply want the help of professionals who know what you don't know, a Community Foundation may be the perfect way to start your adventure as a modern philanthropist. The giving landscape is constantly changing, and a Community Foundation can give you access to the flood of new information that is available—and help you assess and put that knowledge into action. The added bonus is that you will be surrounded by other enthusiastic givers in your own community.

Every giving tool has its own features and benefits, and pros and cons. Even if you are a bona fide do-it-yourselfer (maybe with a multitool on your belt!), this may be one of those times in life when working with a professional can make the difference between a job that's done, and a job that's done *right*.

Remember Linda? She had made giving a priority, but she was diving into the process with no real strategy. After exploring the menu of options together, we were able to create a multi-year strategy that not only felt right to her from a giving perspective, but that would also enable her to give more than she had anticipated in the decades ahead. Armed with her 'giving multitool,' she was able to refine her strategy, including choosing precisely what, where, and when to give to bring her plan to life.

Just like Linda, you now have the information and knowledge you need to take the first steps in your giving journey. You know how giving can change your life and the lives of others. You know how to create a strategy that is aligned with your personal values and goals. And you know which tools are available and why it makes sense to choose one tool over another. The next step is to put all of that knowledge into action by setting your giving budget and choosing the tools for the job.

EXERCISE:

Tackle the nitty gritty

Your giving budget and the tools you choose to support your giving strategy will both influence the level of impact you are able to create. The following exercises are designed to help you begin to develop a concrete giving strategy and choose the tools that are best suited to your goals.

Activity I—Determine your giving budget to be sure your philanthropy is supported by and integrated with your overall wealth management plan.

Activity J—Select giving tools that are aligned with your needs, goals, and giving strategy.

I

DETERMINE YOUR GIVING BUDGET

It is a personal decision to determine how much to give to your focus areas compared to reserving resources for you and your family's present and future needs. This exercise will help you determine your charitable giving budget for the next three years.

The goal is to focus on proactive giving in the focus areas you identified in Chapter 3. The first step is to categorize and distribute your contributions into three buckets:

1. **Proactive giving** includes contributions to organizations working on your selected causes.
2. **Reactive giving** includes contributions to personal requests from family and friends to support their selected causes.
3. **Emergency giving** includes contributions to disaster and emergency relief funds, or dire situations that emerge from unexpected policy changes.

Instructions: Part 1

Answer the following questions to explore how much you want your giving budget to be, and how you want to allocate your budget to each giving category. You may want to involve your financial advisor in the discussion to ensure your strategy is aligned with your overall financial plan. Note that you may choose to skip questions that aren't relevant to you.

How much do you wish to allocate to giving in the next year? Over the next three years?

_____

_____

_____

_____

_____

_____

_____

What future financial situations or developments could affect how much you allocate to giving?

_____

_____

_____

_____

_____

_____

_____

_____

_____

What are the potential tax considerations for your
different time horizons?

_____

_____

_____

_____

_____

_____

_____

_____

Given your current financial circumstances, could you
think about allocating more?

_____

_____

_____

_____

_____

_____

Are you in a position to consider giving appreciated assets as part of your giving plan?

_____

_____

_____

_____

_____

_____

_____

_____

How have you thought about allocating assets for the next generation?

_____

_____

_____

_____

_____

_____

_____

Would you like to revisit your allocation in the future?
If so, when?

_____

_____

_____

_____

_____

_____

_____

How much are you setting aside as your total giving
budget for the next 3 years?

_____

_____

_____

_____

_____

_____

_____

Instructions: Part 2

The next step is to determine how you would like to allocate your total giving budget across the three categories: proactive, reactive, and emergency giving. Use the chart below to indicate your allocations. Adjust each amount until the distribution feels right to you.

Total Giving Budget	3-Year Budget		Year 1		Year 2		Year 3	
	$ Amnt.	%	$ Amnt.	%	$ Amnt.	%	$ Amnt.	%
Proactive Giving includes contributions to organizations working on your selected causes								
Reactive Giving includes contributions to personal requests from family and friends to support their selected causes								
Emergency Giving includes contributions to disaster and emergency relief funds, or dire situations that emerge from unexpected policy changes								

J
SELECT YOUR GIVING TOOLS

Philanthropic vehicles—or giving tools—provide a structure for you to carry out your giving plan. This exercise will help you identify which giving tools are best suited to your personal, financial, and philanthropic preferences. Keep in mind that you can achieve your giving objectives through any vehicle. The goal here is to ensure that you select the vehicle or combination of vehicles that best aligns with your broader needs.

Instructions

Review the list of considerations below and write down your thoughts. This list is not intended to be exhaustive, but rather to spur deeper thinking to help drive your decisions. It is highly recommended that you work with your financial advisor to ensure the giving vehicles you choose are the best available to address your giving budget, preferences, and goals.

Anonymity: Do you prefer to give anonymously, or do you prefer your giving to be public?

_____

_____

_____

Control: Do you want to retain total control over granting decisions?

_____

_____

_____

Distribution: Would you want a vehicle with an annual distribution requirement in place to keep your giving in action?

_____

_____

_____

Family involvement: Do you want your family members involved in giving decisions?

_____

_____

_____

Locale: Do you want your giving to support your local community? Are international issues a priority?

_____

_____

_____

Impact investments: Do you want to make investments that generate both social and financial return, such as requiring ESG (environmental, social, and governance) criteria to screen potential investments?

_____

_____

_____

Timing & perpetuity: Do you prefer to give while you are living, after your death, or both? Do you want the structure of your giving to exist in perpetuity?

_____

_____

_____

Political contributions: Do you want to make political donations and engage in lobbying? Direct political contributions are not tax-deductible, though some lobbying and advocacy can be, depending on a number of factors. Seek further professional advice if politics is a priority issue for you.

_____

_____

_____

Public disclosure: Are you willing to submit separate tax records that make a record of your giving available to the public?

_____

_____

_____

Tax implications: Are tax implications important to your choice of vehicle?

_____

_____

_____

Growth potential: Are you seeking to create a philanthropic investment that increases over time?

_____

_____

_____

Administrative support: Are you willing and able to invest your time and effort on an ongoing basis and hire paid staff for your vehicle?

_____

_____

_____

Ranking: Of the considerations listed above, list the three that are most important to you. These will help drive your selections and choose the most appropriate giving tools for you.

1:_____

2:_____

3:_____

CHAPTER 5

From Moment to Movement

"This is not a moment, it's the movement."
— *Lin-Manuel Miranda in the musical 'Hamilton'*

Giving can be a moment.

But today's givers have the power to take giving to a whole new level.

To make it bigger. Stronger. More impactful.

To create a *movement* that changes the world.

A moment of charity is a moment of clarity. It's an important act.

But being a modern philanthropist is more.

It's an identity. An attitude. A way of living.

Are you ready to start a movement?

Spread the Fire!

"The tipping point is that magic moment
when an idea, trend,
or social behavior crosses a threshold,
tips, and spreads like wildfire."
— *Malcolm Gladwell, 'The Tipping Point:*
How Little Things Can Make a Big Difference'

You have an incredible power to influence others—whether you recognize it or not.

If you're a parent, you've probably had to deal with the challenge of trying to keep your kids from hanging out with the 'wrong crowd.' And you know precisely why. The wrong crowd can influence kids to change their own behavior—for better or for worse.

The same, of course, is true for adults. When we spend our time with honest, caring, giving people, we want to rise up and emulate their greatness. We want to be better ourselves. The opposite can also be true. (Though as adults, we hopefully choose the wiser path more often than not!)

As a modern philanthropist, now is the time to influence others in the best way possible. This is your chance to lift up others. Make this part of your giving strategy and you can exponentially grow your impact—and even help others reap the many rewards of giving themselves.

Inspire the Next Generation

In Chapter 1, I told the story of Victor Klein, a generous giver who wanted his name proudly displayed on the walls of the synagogue for his grandchildren to see. His goal was to inspire them long after he was gone. His approach was right for him, but it certainly isn't the only way to motivate future generations of givers.

How can you inspire your children, grandchildren, and great-grandchildren to become lifelong philanthropists—even after you're gone? Here are some strategies that have worked for other givers.

Talk about giving.

In a society that has made it taboo to talk about money, it's easy to overlook the importance of talking about giving. It doesn't help that talking about giving is sometimes seen as bragging (a la Ted Danson on *Curb Your Enthusiasm*!). But simply talking about how, where, and why you give is one of the best ways to inspire giving in your own family. Have you created a Donor-Advised Fund? Talk about it. Did you help someone on the street today? Did you donate appreciated stock to a cause that matters to you? Did you take action to double a gift by signing up for your company's corporate matching program? Talk about it. Sharing your story—either with each person individually or as a group—is one of the most successful ways to create a giving tradition that lasts for generations.

Be a giving guide—or find one.

If you have school-aged children, work with them to identify ways they can give their time, talent, or treasure. When we encouraged our daughter to join the Young Philanthropists, we hit the jackpot. Not only did she discover the joys of giving, but we also got to know Nancy Chase better. Nancy co-founded the group, and her vision was an amazing gift for Beaue, and for me and my wife, Jeanne. Nancy's passion for her work at Families Forward, a local charity that helps people on the edge of poverty get a roof over their heads and food on the table, was infectious. Through her and her amazingly generous family, we all learned new paths for giving, how to give more effectively, and the personal rewards of giving.

Whenever guiding a young person, it helps to be as clear and concise as possible—and to focus on the ways they interact with the world around them. Generally, that means social media, YouTube, and a variety of other channels for online communication. Point out the hashtag #philanthropy on Instagram and Twitter—and then sit down together to check out the latest stories. You'll both be inspired by the innovative ways people around the world are giving to others.

Get everyone involved.

The more you can include other family members in the giving process, the more likely they are to continue to give in the future. As part of our Giving Circle, all of the families in the group encouraged their kids to be active in the conversations and the giving decisions. Every member, no matter how young or old, shared their ideas, perspectives, and opinions. And we chose where to give *together*. Consider creating a Giving Circle for your own family. Meet a few times a year to talk about the giving budget. Ask each person to share their own ideas about where they would like to give, and then choose your causes together. Making each person an equal and active participant can create a passion for giving in everyone.

Another great option is to create a Donor-Advised Fund in the names of your children or grandchildren, and then provide the initial funding. By giving them the means to give, you can generate a habit of giving—and give them a tool to support their philanthropy for decades and generations to come.

See Chapter 4 to learn more about Giving Circles and Donor-Advised Funds.

Write an Ethical Will.

According to Jewish tradition, every human soul carries one small piece of God's message into the world. An Ethical Will is a wonderful tool you can use to share that message with your family—including your values, experiences, life lessons, and why giving matters to you.

Your letter can include anything you want it to. What's most important is that it tells the people you love your story. What has life taught you? What are your most cherished memories? What were your greatest triumphs—and your worst failures? What has been the greatest wisdom you've learned in life (so far)? What's your unique message you want to share with your family and the world?

This can be as fun and creative as you choose. Some people include family photographs or recipes that have been passed down from generation to generation. Some make videos to add to or even replace a written document. Others expand their ethical 'letters' into full-blown memoirs. You can include anything that helps paint a picture of your life for generations to come. As a modern philanthropist, one important piece of your story is what compelled you to become a giver, why you choose to support certain causes, and how you hope your descendants will continue the tradition of giving.

Pay It Forward

I've shared the story about offering the young man in Laguna Beach $100. I had just wanted to help in a small way, but for him, the gift was greater than I could have imagined—literally making it possible for him "to live like a normal human being" for the next few days. The only thing I asked in return was for him to pay it forward; to share it with others who also needed help.

At a diner in New Jersey, a waitress overheard two customers, both firefighters, talking about the warehouse fire they had just battled through the night. At the end of their breakfast, instead of a bill, they received a note from their server thanking them for their service. The men later learned that the waitress was struggling to raise funds to buy a wheelchair accessible van for her paralyzed father. They paid it forward quickly, raising $56,000 in just three days to cover the expense.

In early December 2020, as another surge of coronavirus was sweeping across the country, an amazing thing happened at a Dairy Queen in Minnesota. With restaurants closed due to the pandemic, cars were lined up for takeout orders at the Dairy Queen drive-through when one customer decided to 'pay it forward' by purchasing the next car's meal. As each new car approached the window, customer after customer was surprised to learn their meal had been paid for—and every single car continued to pay it forward in a giving chain that lasted for more than 900 cars and three full days.

Paying it forward is such a simple act. And yet it can serve as a powerful inspiration to others. Givers who routinely pay it forward say it has changed their lives.

The #BlazeItForward exercise at the end of Chapter 3 was focused on the rewards of giving and how the action made you feel. But the potential of paying it forward reaches far beyond you (the giver) and the single recipient of your gift. As each new car pulled up to that Dairy Queen window, they were surprised by the small gift of a pre-paid meal. But when the staff told them how long the chain had been going, many people burst into tears, overwhelmed by what was happening. As the wave of giving continued, it grew. And grew. Until the giving became more than a simple gesture of goodwill. Suddenly, it was an important symbol of a community coming together in a time of need.

That is the true spirit of giving.

Give All Year Long

'The season of giving.' It's a phrase we've all come to know. The combination of the holidays and year-end tax planning has made the time between Thanksgiving and New Year's Eve *the* time for giving. At Thanksgiving, food banks across the US are flooded with offers to help. Financial donations pour in, and people volunteer in droves to come serve meals to people in need. Each December, charities receive almost a third of their annual donations in a single month. And 12% of all giving happens in the last 3 days of the year.[16]

But how much more could we achieve—and how much impact could we create—if the 'season of giving' lasted all year round? It's a goal that finally seems to be in sight.

The Tax Cuts and Jobs Act (TCJA) of 2017 changed how most of us are taxed on charitable donations, reducing the marginal tax benefit of giving to charity by more than 30% in 2018, and raising the after-tax cost of donating by about 7%. But despite the fact that giving actually 'costs' more (about *twice* as much as it cost 40 years ago), the data shows that our giving nature has prevailed. According to Giving USA, Americans contributed nearly $471 billion to charitable causes in 2020, despite an economic downturn that impacted the income of

---

[16] Source: Neon One.

millions. Data gathered from #GivingTuesday showed a 29% jump in giving over 2019, with 34.8 million people contributing a total of $2.47 billion in a single day.

When people are in need, givers take action.

But whether it hits the headlines or not, the need is always there. Every year—not just in 2020. Every month—not just in December. Every day—not just in the last three days of the year.

It's time to transform the 'season of giving' into year-round action. If you want to feed the homeless, volunteer your time on one or more of the *other* 364 days of the year—not only on Thanksgiving. If you want to give money to a cause, schedule a monthly gift rather than waiting until December. Any gift, any time, is appreciated, but giving when it's not 'the season' is a great way to help charities do good throughout the year.

Get Vocal

Gina Martin was one of the first activists to use the full potential of the internet to get vocal. In her book, *Be the Change: A Toolkit for the Activist in You*, she describes herself as a "regular working-class person." She had no experience in politics and had no idea where to start when she began her campaign to make 'upskirting' (taking photos up a woman's skirt without her consent) illegal in the UK. Using the power of social media, she collected more than 110,000 signatures on her petition, and eventually was invited to meet with the British justice minister about her cause. The issue was debated in parliament and became law in 2019.

Charles (Chuck) Feeney made a fortune as cofounder of Duty Free Shoppers, the retail stores found in every major airport. His mission was to give it all away—anonymously— and he broadcast his message of 'Giving While Living' to anyone who would listen. It took him decades to give away more than $8 billion to a variety of charities, universities, and foundations around the world, and today the former billionaire is officially broke. (According to a recent interview with *Forbes*, he couldn't be happier!) It was Chuck Feeney who served as the inspiration for The Giving Pledge.

----

*To learn more about The Giving Pledge,
see Chapter 2.*

Just three days after the deadliest school shooting in US history[17], the survivors of the Marjory Stoneman Douglas High School in Parkland, Florida, led a rally to speak out against gun violence and advocate for gun control. They called out the many politicians who receive campaign contributions from the NRA, and they raised their voices for change. A month later, the group organized the March for Our Lives in support of greater gun control, a Washington, D.C. event that drew the personal and financial support of a host of celebrities, including

----

[17] As of December 2020.

George Clooney, Scooter Braun, and Oprah Winfrey, and attracted hundreds of thousands of attendees. The actions of this vocal group sparked a global push toward stricter regulations and gun laws in the US.

Greta Thunberg was born in 2003 into a world threatened by climate change. Distraught that her parents' generation was doing little to save the world of her future, she began the school climate strike in Sweden at age 15—her first step as a global climate activist. Within a year, she was recognized around the world. While still in her teens, she was an invited speaker at the UN Climate Action Summit, the United Nations Climate Change Conference, the World Economic Forum, and the European Parliament's Environment Committee in 2020. As the threats of climate change accelerated in 2021, her message resonated even deeper. Thunberg has said that her first inspiration came from the students in Parkland and their refusal to return to school without the safety of gun control.

These events may be the extremes, but they are proof that getting vocal is a key to inspiring others—and to creating a movement of change. Gina Martin inspired parliament to make upskirting illegal. Chuck Feeney inspired the founders of The Giving Pledge. The Parkland survivors' actions inspired Greta Thunberg, and her work inspired the founders of student climate networks around the world.

What action can you take today to create a movement for change? Whatever your passion may be, as a modern philanthropist, you have the power to make a difference. No matter how old or young you are. No matter how much or how little you have to give. The time to get vocal is now.

Just Ask

Sometimes the best way to inspire others to give is incredibly simple: Just ask.

When I first met with Alisa, she was volunteering for a few causes in the local community and our children's school. I didn't know her well, and I had no idea if she was a giver, but I had the feeling that she was the kind of person that got things done.

We got to know Alisa over time, and we were invited to her 50th birthday party, which happened to be on New Year's Eve. In lieu of gifts, she asked her guests to donate to charity. The following year, she hosted a huge party at a nearby hotel. Again, she asked her guests to give to others in lieu of birthday gifts, but this time her request was more specific: she asked everyone to give to a local charity, Court Appointed Special Advocates (CASA), that serves severely abused, neglected, and abandoned children, many of whom are in foster care. At the event, she presented a slide show to tell the story of the young woman she had 'adopted' through the CASA program. Alisa's party guests contributed over $15,000 to the program that night. And who knows... perhaps she inspired others to be more active themselves. Because she had the courage to ask.

It was at that moment at the party that I realized how many opportunities I had missed to simply ask.

Asking isn't always easy. It can feel like you're putting people on the spot, or that you're asking for something for *you* (as illogical as that may be). If it's hard for you to ask, here are three simple tips that can help make it easier—both for you and the person you're asking to give:

■ *Tell a story about how your own gift has made a difference.*

Whether you gave time, talent, or treasure, share details about a specific way your gift was used based on information you have about the charity. The more personal your story can be, the better. Alisa told the story about her experience with one person she helped at CASA. Because it was personal to her, it became personal to everyone listening. That made them happy to give.

■ *Do your research.*

Be prepared to answer questions about the charity you want to support. What is their mission? How do they spend their resources? What kind of impact have they had in the past or hope to have in the future? (For any questions you can't answer, point to the Charity Navigator website as a resource.)

■ *Share your own experience.*

One of the most powerful ways to ask others for support is to share why you give to an organization yourself. Why did you first decide to give? How did you choose the recipient of your gift? What have been your own rewards of giving?

Not everyone you ask will take action and give, but by sharing your passion for giving, telling your story, and just asking for help, you can help build momentum and create a whole new level of change.

Create a Movement

Taking action to become a giver yourself is the first step in becoming a modern philanthropist. The next step is to create energy around giving by encouraging others to share their own time, talent, treasure—or anything else they are willing to give to help others.

Many celebrities are active philanthropists, using their public profiles and voices to encourage others to give. "The world's best-known philan- thropist," Bono, U2's lead singer, has used his fortune and influence to drive support for third-world debt relief and battling the HIV/AIDS pandemic for more than 20 years. Angelina Jolie is known for helping refugees and survivors of natural disasters, even joining field missions in dozens of countries. Miley Cyrus has been named the "most charitable celebrity" thanks to her work with children in the US and Haiti. Leonar- do DiCaprio, a UN Messenger of Peace for the Climate and founder of the Leonardo DiCaprio Foundation, has dedicated much of his life to protecting the world's oceans, wildlife, and forests. The list of celebrity givers includes a who's-who of the top names in entertainment, including Beyoncé, Oprah Winfrey, Justin Bieber, Shawn Mendez, George Clooney, Luke Combs, Taylor Swift, Selena Gomez, Nicki Minaj, Ben Affleck, Kylie Jenner, Betty White, Katy Perry, The Weeknd, Matthew McConaughey, Matt Damon, and Scarlet Johansson.

The Ice Bucket Challenge

If you spent any time on social media back in 2014, you need no introduction to the ALS Ice Bucket Challenge. The 'challenge' was simple: participants had a bucket of ice water poured over their heads—either by themselves or someone else—and posted a video of their reaction to social media. They would then challenge others to participate in the challenge.

The goal was to raise awareness and funds for amyotrophic lateral sclerosis, commonly called ALS or Lou Gehrig's disease. And it created a massive movement. Because it was fun (watching people's reactions to the wave of ice water was great entertainment) and unique, it caught on like wildfire, raising over $220 million for the cause in just two months. Some participants were celebrities. Most were just everyday people who came together to make a difference.

There are many ways to create a movement. Find what works for you—and run with it!

During the COVID-19 pandemic, celebrity philanthropists gave in a variety of ways. Dolly Parton helped fund Moderna's research that led to the pharmaceutical company's COVID-19 vaccine. Celebrity chef Guy Fieri raised over $21.5 million to help struggling restaurant workers. U2 donated €10 million (more than $12 million) to help provide equipment to frontline workers.

But the giving that may have mattered most was driven by people like you and me. The far-from-famous people who ordered takeout from their local restaurants, checked on their elderly neighbors, and contributed to local food banks. The middle school woodworking teacher in New Jersey who filled his living room with 3D printers to make PPE masks for frontline workers. The teenage brothers who launched a free, online tutoring service for younger kids struggling with online learning. And the individuals and families who donated almost $12 billion to coronavirus relief funds in the first 6 months of 2020 alone—more than all of the donations combined received in response to the 9/11 attacks, hurricanes Harvey and Sandy, and the 2008 financial crisis.[18] The challenge now is to continue to build on that momentum to create lasting change.

If there was one silver lining to the pandemic, it is that everyday givers emerged and came to the rescue. These givers are the new face of philanthropy. They aren't rich or famous. But when they saw that other people needed help, they acted.

They are your friends. They are your neighbors. They are *you*.

Now is the time for giving to change your life.

---

[18] Source: Candid and the Center for Disaster Philanthropy.

EXERCISE:

SET THE STAGE FOR A GIVING MOVEMENT

You don't need to be a celebrity or billionaire to create your own giving movement.

Activity K—Involve your family to build enthusiasm around your own giving and inspire multiple generations of modern philanthropists.

Activity L—Make a giving pledge that reflects your own desires as a modern philanthropist.

K
INVOLVE YOUR FAMILY

Charitable giving presents an opportunity to involve your family in one of life's most fulfilling activities: giving back. You can engage family members in philanthropy in many ways, including asking them to advise or assist you in developing philanthropic goals, creating and implementing a giving strategy, launching family members on their own giving trajectory, and more. Who is included in your family is entirely up to you. Involving your family can take multiple forms, from involving them in decision-making to preparing for eventual succession.

Instructions: Part 1

Review the following questions and write down your thoughts. You don't have to answer all of the questions, but it is recommended that you consider each one carefully before reaching out to family members.

What motivates you to involve your family in your charitable giving?

_____

_____

_____

_____

_____

_____

What obstacles could arise from involving your family in your charitable giving plans?

_____

_____

_____

_____

_____

_____

Is your giving a continuation of your family's legacy or something you are starting?

_____

_____

_____

_____

_____

_____

_____

What values do you want to ensure get translated through your shared giving?

_____

_____

_____

_____

_____

_____

_____

Are you looking to engage your family in an ongoing way with all decision making, or do you want your family members to help carry out your vision and decisions?

_____

_____

_____

_____

_____

_____

_____

Are there giving decisions for which you want others to have full discretion?

_____

_____

_____

_____

_____

_____

_____

Are there giving decisions that you would like to make collaboratively? If yes, how would you like these decisions to be made (e.g., by majority vote)?

_____

_____

_____

_____

_____

_____

_____

Which family members do you want to engage in your charitable giving? (List them here, and you can determine specific roles in the next activity.)

_____

_____

_____

_____

_____

_____

_____

Will some family members be upset if you do not include them? How might you communicate your decision to them?

_____

_____

_____

_____

_____

_____

_____

_____

_____

_____

_____

_____

Instructions: Part 2

Philanthropy is an opportunity to bring your family together around a common goal, communicate values across generations, and develop a sense of social responsibility in the next generation. Below are three suggested activities to introduce the next generation to giving.

Start a conversation about giving with younger family members. Share your reasons for giving, including personal stories whenever possible. Invite their feedback. Ask what causes are important to them and how they would choose to give if they were empowered to make their own giving decisions. Reflect on the conversation below.

_____

_____

_____

_____

_____

_____

_____

_____

Host a family dinner or meeting with the next generation to discuss charitable giving. One way to begin the discussion might be to engage with an exploration of the causes that are most important to each person using the exercises in this book. Ask each person to identify their top cause and write it down below, as well as any new ideas or insights from your time together that may impact your own giving strategy.

_____

_____

_____

_____

_____

_____

_____

_____

_____

_____

_____

_____

_____

L(ast)
MAKE A GIVING PLEDGE

Warren Buffet, Bill Gates, and Melinda French Gates created The Giving Pledge to encourage the wealthiest people in the world to dedicate the majority of their wealth to giving back. My own dream is to see this idea spread to include anyone and everyone who has the capacity to give to others—the non-billionaires and non-millionaires who may not have acquired massive wealth, but who still have so much to give.
A giving pledge for the modern philanthropist.

Instructions
Create your pledge today by writing down your answers to the following questions:

Why do you want to give?

_____

_____

_____

_____

_____

_____

What, where, and when do you plan to give (use the exercises in this book to guide you)?

_____

_____

_____

_____

_____

_____

_____

How do you plan to give (include the giving tools that best support your strategy)?

_____

_____

_____

_____

_____

_____

_____

Once you have written your pledge, talk to a financial advisor, Community Foundation representative, or other experienced giver to create a concrete giving strategy based on your resources and giving goals.

The action you take as a modern philanthropist matters. Get ready to change the world—and change your life.

Afterword

Writing *Giving* has been my way of giving back and encouraging others to give freely and strategically. As I shared in Chapter 2, the act of giving helped me find my own purpose again following my son Blaze's death in 2018. I was hesitant to write about my son's death here. It's such a deeply personal experience, and I was afraid that the telling of it would bring sadness rather than inspiration. But my wife, Jeanne, encouraged me, reminding me that Blaze's death has inspired so much goodness—and so much giving. Here is our story in a nutshell. I hope that reading it doesn't bring sadness. Instead, my hope is that it inspires you to give, whenever and wherever you can, to make the world we live in a better place for all.

When our son Blaze died, it was no ordinary death. Blaze was murdered. He disappeared on January 2, 2018, and he was found dead in a park near our home 8 long days later, on January 10. A former classmate was arrested and charged with a hate crime. It was then that charitable giving took a front seat in our lives.

Those 8 days in between Blaze's disappearance and when he was finally found were the worst days of my life. We searched desperately for information about where Blaze may have gone and, if he was dead, where his body could be. We had a long dining room table in our home topped with 6 computer stations that were being piloted by amazing friends, each working madly looking for leads of any kind. Our house was full of people and nervous energy until midnight every night, and it all began again each morning at 7:00 when Dr. Rocky Goldberg would show up with bagels on his way to work in the trauma department at Mission Hospital.

We were the trauma department of Foothill Ranch.

*On day 7 of our search, I looked around at the generous friends and ac-
quaintances sitting at our table, each staring into a glowing computer
screen searching for clues. At my side was Wendy Arenson, the Executive
Director of the Jewish Community Foundation of Orange County where
I served as Chairman of the Board. I turned to Wendy and asked if we
should do something big on our 'Help us Find Blaze Bernstein' Facebook
page. She turned to me and asked, "What could we possibly do that we're
not doing already?"*

*But I had already formed the beginnings of a plan in my mind. So many
people were reaching out and wanting to help us, but I knew there was
nothing much more to do. We were searching everywhere and using every
possible resource. Jeanne and I both recognized that this tragedy had set us
squarely in the face of a great opportunity to create a wave of philanthropic
giving. I looked at Wendy and I suddenly knew what to do. "I'm going to ask
the thousands of followers on our Facebook page to give to people who really
need help—to support a local charity and create something good."*

*Wendy thought it was a great idea. Over the next half hour, we narrowed
down our options and chose The Orangewood Foundation, an organization focused on helping youth in need, foster children, and the homeless.
I immediately posted a note on the Facebook page asking people to make
a difference in someone's life by donating to the foundation. Less than an
hour later, we were told that the server at Orangewood was down—the
system couldn't handle the massive number of donations that were pouring
in online. The wave of giving we had hoped for had begun!*

*It was the first thing that had felt good in almost a week. More than
$16,000 had been donated in Blaze's name. That was a moment of truth*

for me and Jeanne. The energy and relief we felt seeing so much giving and kindness was a tremendous distraction from our grief. It gave us purpose. It gave us a tangible result. And it gave us <u>hope</u>. It was a game changer in our lives.

The next morning, the coroner called to tell us they had identified Blaze's body. He had been buried in a shallow grave at the park not far from our house—right next to the elementary school Blaze had attended as a child. There are no words I can write to express the devastation we felt. It isn't possible to share our story without crying. We finally had answers. We could finally have a funeral. But we didn't know what was going to happen next in our lives.

Thankfully, our amazing friends did. The group that had assembled at our house every day—lawyers, medical doctors, therapists, public relations professionals, marketing professionals, website developers—all knew how to help us take the next step forward. Our dear friend David Thalberg listened as we shared our dream of creating a wave of giving to honor Blaze's legacy of kindness. We wanted to use this platform to achieve philanthropy on a scale we had never dreamed was possible. David volunteered to make our vision come true, taking over our PR efforts and helping us craft a plan to launch a movement we call #BlazeItForward. It was our first step toward healing and rebuilding our lives without Blaze.

There is nothing that will kill your hope in humanity like losing a child through the hateful act of another human. But from the moment we learned of Blaze's death, we did not respond with hate or anger. We knew in our hearts that revenge would not bring us any reward or fulfillment—and that even 'justice' (if there really is such a thing) wouldn't bring Blaze back. Instead of seeking revenge, we chose to rise above our grief and respond in the most meaningful way we could: by using the moment to elevate ourselves and others to a higher place. It's what Blaze would have wanted.

Jeanne and I have lived all of our lives trying to improve the human condition and wanting to leave the world better off for our having been here. The thought that someone could kill our child in a violent hateful way went beyond anything that we could ever have imagined. Something like this could have destroyed us, making us as hateful and vengeful as Blaze's murderer. We found a better path. #BlazeItForward has become our way of sharing the importance and value of giving. This book is part of that movement. I hope that by sharing the 'why, what, how, and when' of becoming a modern philanthropist, I can make Blaze's legacy live on. I hope you'll join me in making that dream come true.

Acknowledgements

Very few football players make it to the 'end zone' in a game, and the same goes for completing and publishing a book. I have many people to thank for assisting and inspiring me to achieve this milestone and share my passion for giving with the world.

Ralph White, you pushed me and held me accountable along the whole journey, and you helped me to understand that possibilities are unlimited. CaroleAnne Hardy, I could not have done this without your incredible talent and help in reshaping my vision into a beautiful, inspirational handbook. Thank you to my wife, Jeanne Pepper, for your out-of-the-box approach to life and your careful review and editing; to our children, Jay, Beaue, and Blaze (z"l), for being my daily inspiration to try to do good and make this world a better place; and to my parents, Richard and Leah Bernstein, for being the ultimate role models for true generosity and tenacity. To my fellow board members at the Isadore C and Penny W Myers Foundation, and to Jay Myers who leads the charge in making an impact on the lives of many, thank you for your inspiration and for making me an advocate for giving. And to Wendy Arenson, Executive Director at the Jewish Community Foundation of Orange County, thank you for your valuable input, your guidance and, most of all, your friendship.

To the entire team at Leisure Capital Management—Marr Leisure, Raymond Robinson, Patrick Maxwell, Christina Todd, Sandra Dick, Avery Wenck, Barbara Salamoff, and John Schaus—thank you for holding me up and making me look good for almost two decades. And thank you to Schwab Charitable for allowing me to share your thoughtful content as the foundation for many of the exercises in this book.

Finally, I dedicate this book to all of my amazing friends, community, and clients. As givers to your families, communities, friends, and strangers in need, you have shown me how to be compassionate and truly change lives. I hope the stories in this book illustrate how such dedication to giving can create a butterfly effect that makes the world a better place for all.

About the Author

Gideon Bernstein has served as a trusted financial advisor to affluent families in Orange County, California, for decades, and he is currently a Principal and Chief Investment Officer at Leisure Capital Management. His passion is working with non-profit boards, families, and private foundations to help them achieve their philanthropic missions. Gideon has served as a board member of numerous charitable organizations and as Vice President of Investments and Chairman of the Board for the Jewish Community Foundation of Orange County. He holds designations as a Chartered Financial Analyst (CFA) and a Chartered Advisor in Philanthropy (CAP). *Giving* is Gideon's first book.

Made in the USA
Las Vegas, NV
01 December 2021

35747942R00109